Camila Batmangheli...
and Kids Comp...

Danny Dor...

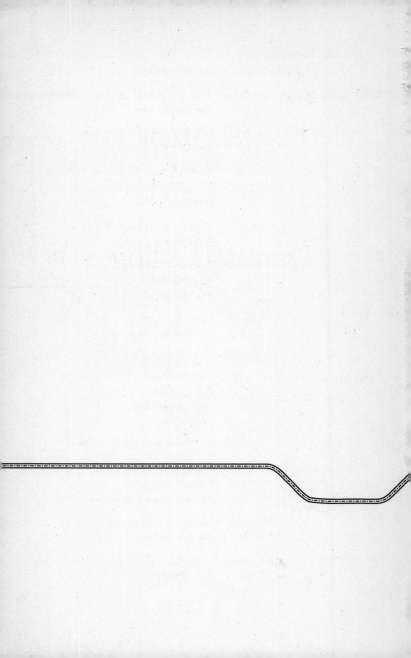

The 32 Stops

Lives on London's Central Line

Danny Dorling

PENGUIN BOOKS

PENGUIN BOOKS

Published by the Penguin Group
Penguin Books Ltd, 80 Strand, London WC2R 0RL, England
Penguin Group (USA) Inc., 375 Hudson Street, New York, New York 10014, USA
Penguin Group (Canada), 90 Eglinton Avenue East, Suite 700, Toronto, Ontario,
Canada M4P 2Y3 (a division of Pearson Penguin Canada Inc.)
Penguin Ireland, 25 St Stephen's Green, Dublin 2, Ireland (a division of Penguin Books Ltd)
Penguin Group (Australia), 707 Collins Street, Melbourne, Victoria 3008, Australia
(a division of Pearson Australia Group Pty Ltd)
Penguin Books India Pvt Ltd, 11 Community Centre, Panchsheel Park, New Delhi – 110 017, India
Penguin Group (NZ), 67 Apollo Drive, Rosedale, Auckland 0632, New Zealand
(a division of Pearson New Zealand Ltd)
Penguin Books (South Africa) (Pty) Ltd, Block D, Rosebank Office Park,
181 Jan Smuts Avenue, Parktown North, Gauteng 2193, South Africa

Penguin Books Ltd, Registered Offices: 80 Strand, London WC2R 0RL, England

www.penguin.com

First published in Penguin Books 2013
002

Set in 11.75/15pt Baskerville MT Std
Typeset by Jouve (UK), Milton Keynes
Printed in England by Clays Ltd, St Ives plc

ISBN: 978-1-846-14560-5

www.greenpenguin.co.uk

Penguin Books is committed to a sustainable
future for our business, our readers and our planet.
This book is made from Forest Stewardship
Council™ certified paper.

ALWAYS LEARNING   **PEARSON**

To Bethan Suyin Thomas, who loves London.

Like the trace of a heartbeat on a cardiac monitor, the Central Line slowly falls south through west London, rises gently through the centre and then flicks up north through the east end of the capital. At the start of the journey life expectancy falls by two months a minute. The train is rapidly crossing many invisible boundaries. Between the first four stations every second spent moving is exactly a day off their lives in terms of how long people living beside the tracks can expect to live.[1] And it is not so much the exercise people take, or how healthily they eat, or whether or not they smoke that matters. It's much more who ends up living here. At the very start of the line those who do better in life end up living, on average, further out from the centre. But luck has a lot to do with where you end up living along the line too, good luck as well as bad luck.

The line is over a century old. Its westernmost station was opened on 2 April 1911, on the very same Sunday that the groundbreaking 1911 Population Census was taken, the first census to make a detailed record of living conditions, main employer and the number of families living in each home. It recorded the industry or services with which the workers of the households were connected, how long couples had been married and how many children were born alive, how many were still alive and how many had died.[2] It was the census from which our current coding of social class was first derived and through which we first recorded our intention to improve infant health.

Everything you are about to read is based on fact. These facts are taken from official records. They come from children's GCSE school exam certificates, from pensioners' death certificates recording the length of life of each and assigning each an underlying cause of mortality. These facts come from censuses and surveys, counts of bankers and tax office estimates of average incomes. They also come from others' descriptions, such as the official summaries of the number of children growing up in poverty in each place. What all these facts do is determine the social gradient between places, in this case between tube stops of the Central Line. They can tell us at which point, and in which aspects of life, we are heading up or down, socially, as we travel west to east, geographically.

Saturday 2 April 2011, West Ruislip, 6.00 a.m.

Exactly a century after the 1911 census was taken, and after the furthest tube line west was opened, a couple are arguing in bed. They are arguing about the census and why they chose to live in West Ruislip.

'Don't forget the baby,' he said.

How could she forget the baby? They'd moved for the baby, for the extra room, for the future. The baby was much more important than the census form. The form that had been sitting by the kitchen sink for a week.

'Someone at work was telling me, only yesterday, that people always forget to add the baby,' he said.

He worked in town, in Islington, he changed at Bank, but in May the office was moving to Pimlico and then he'd change at Oxford Circus.[3] That was the great thing about the Central Line: it didn't matter if you changed your job or if your job changed its offices – everything was always roughly the same distance away, measured by travel time if not miles. They'd moved here because it was safe and getting safer. Crime in the ward had dropped by 13 per cent in the last year (it would drop by another 15 per cent this year). Such crime as there was could mostly be classified as petty antisocial behaviour. Almost all of it took place in just a few streets. He told her which streets.[4]

'That's why we didn't choose to live there,' he said.[5]

He liked statistics. He worked for the Office for National Statistics. It took him exactly

35 minutes to do most of the *Daily Telegraph* crossword, leaving precisely a minute to sit down in his seat and precisely a minute to get up.

Babies do not work to timetables. Babies do not derive pleasure from being told that their parents have mortgaged themselves beyond the hilt to secure them a premier postcode, a place where the average GCSE score is 356 points.[6] He had annoyed her intensely when he decided he needed to explain that particular school statistic to her as they were looking at possible semis to buy. Again his colleague at work had explained it to him.

'The average child in London is awarded 337 points for its GCSEs, but the average for West Ruislip is 356 points. Although our child won't be average; our child will be very clever.'

He was going to go on to try to explain how GCSE result scores are calculated, but he had lost her attention.

'Babies get left off census forms all the time,' he had said, just last night, as she was falling asleep. Her nightmare had been about forgetting the baby, not being able to add up the numbers, finding she was living in a place because of the numbers, because of the numbers about the neighbours.

'And it's 90 per cent white,' he told her.[7]

'We shouldn't be choosing where to live because of that,' she said.

'No,' he agreed.

Exactly three minutes down the line is Ruislip Gardens, GCSE point average of 353.

'Almost slipping by a whole grade in one subject,' he told her, as she rolled her eyes.

'I don't care about the schools,' she said. 'I don't care about the crime. I don't care about the numbers. I just want to get one decent night's sleep.' But she did care, not as much as him, but enough to agree with him about where to live.

Ruislip Gardens, 6.30 a.m.

'The thing about three-year-olds is that they think it's waking-up time when it's light,' she tried to explain.

'But it's Saturday,' he moaned. 'When am I going to get my Saturdays back?'

'We're a post-industrial family,' she replied. 'Saturdays are workdays now.'

'Where did you get "post-industrial" from?' he asked.

'The council,' she replied.[8] 'Almost five times as many people living here are post-industrial families than in the rest of the borough.'

'What's a post-industrial family?' he asked wearily, thinking back to the days of lie-ins.

'Most households are traditional families with school-age children. They generally live in three-bedroom terraced houses,' she read (from the council pamphlet 'A focus on Manor Ward'). 'Five thousand, two hundred and three of us, almost half the neighbourhood, are post-industrial.'

'What's so post-industrial about living in a terrace?' he asked.

'Search me,' she replied. 'But look, here, there's a chart of schools – Ruislip Manor is not doing badly, over 80 per cent get Level 4 in both English and Maths at Key Stage Two.'[9]

'It's not as good as West Ruislip,' he said.

'West Ruislip's results are slipping,' she replied.

'So are Manor's,' he said.

'Look, it's better than South Ruislip,' she pointed out.

'But South Ruislip's getting better,' he retorted.

'Oh, that's only one year,' she said, exasperated.

'The most recent year,' he replied, then asked, sarcastically, 'which schools do you think drive these numbers?'

'Why are we arguing about this at 6.30 in the morning?' she sighed.

'Teddy's stuck in plop-plop,' announced the three-year-old.

That's why we're arguing, she thought, as the father of the three-year-old rushed to the toilet to save Teddy. Luckily the three-year-old's thumbs were too weak to work the flush.

'Look,' he said, blow-drying Teddy, 'it's not as good as West Ruislip here, but it's better than South Ruislip. We're in between. Everything is in between. House prices, schools, everything. That's why we're here.'

'And my folks,' she reminded him. 'Don't forget where most of the deposit came from.'

'We owe them.'

South Ruislip, 7.00 a.m.

'No, you haven't got school today. Go down and watch telly,' he pleaded.

She was only just six years old and wasn't very good with days of the week yet. He was tired; his wife was still asleep, but waking. It was getting easier, he told himself. But why didn't she know Saturday came after Friday? She knew how to use the three remote controls it took to make the flat screen work downstairs. But she didn't know the days of the week. What were they teaching them at that school?

His wife worried more than he did. They were in a good borough after all, but they were on the edge of the good bit.

Cigarette, he thought. Had he muttered it out loud? 'Later,' he told himself, when the kid wouldn't notice. It bugged him when she said he smelt of smoke. At work, too, it was getting harder to smoke; he had to go down the road now, not just outside.

A fifth, he thought. A fifth of people smoked where they lived. His wife had drawn the map. She worked for the borough. She told him she'd chosen the brown tobacco-stain shades on its key especially for him. She didn't smoke.

'Look, Dot,' he said. She was called Dorothy and hated the name. 'It's because we live on the tube line. Less than one in six smoke in Ickenham, Eastcote and Northwood. They're all just a mile or so away from the tube. So they must be more relaxed places.[10] Look,' he said, warming to his theme. 'It's the stress of being a commuter.'

'You're not a commuter. And anyway, it's a "synthetic estimate",' she said, making quotation marks with her fingers. 'It's been made up by the company we pay to get the data to draw the maps. Nobody really knows how many people smoke round here.'

She'd got all clever like that when he started to be shirty. He thought it had become worse since they retitled her group the 'Corporate Performance & Intelligence Team'.

Imagine calling her team 'intelligence'. It wasn't as if they were fighting a war, was it? And since when had the London Borough of Hillingdon become a 'corporation' that had to 'perform'? Last year her group had been the plain old 'Policy Team'. Last year's report hadn't included any annoying tobacco-stained maps of smoking.[11] And last year she'd pointed out just how much South Ruislip's primary schools were improving, just as the little one was about to go. This year she was worried. The ward had slipped back, especially at Key Stage 2. West Ruislip was doing better than South Ruislip.

'We should think of moving,' she said.

'You need to get that promotion,' he said.

'I need more qualifications,' she replied. 'That's why I'm meeting that lecturer at Tottenham Court Road at 3.00 this afternoon.'

Cigarette, he thought. He could hear that his daughter had figured out how to get the DVD player working.

What was the real reason for his wife meeting a lecturer on a Saturday at Tottenham Court Road? What was the lecturer doing working on a Saturday afternoon?

Northolt, 7.30 a.m.

A DVD player didn't cost anything. Of course
they had to have a DVD player. The boy
was nine. He couldn't tell his friends that
they couldn't watch a DVD here. It wasn't
as if she wasn't working. And she was getting
Tax Credits. It was just that she was working
part-time, twenty hours in a week, most
weeks, getting about £10 an hour, £200 a
week (£800 a month, just under ten grand
a year). Child Tax Credits gave her another
£56 a week for the boy.[12] Then she got Child
Benefit, £20 a week. However, she was about
to lose £20 a week because of the Housing
Benefit cuts.[13] That was like losing the Child
Benefit. Every week! She had to find another
£20. Every week! That was like not buying the
cheapest DVD player. Every week!

And £20 a week is £80 a month, is £1,000 a
year, is £10,000 by the time he is nineteen.
That's a lot of jeans. It is a lot of money to her
and to him. But they had to stay in the area.
It was a nice area. But it's a Labour ward,

a Labour area; it has a Labour MP. It's not as if she's living somewhere posh.

She could save the money by stopping having the Internet at home and selling her computer. He needs her computer and the Internet for his homework – there is a 'club' at school for that (but he calls it 'chav club'). The school was not that great, but she could just afford to live here, and she could get work here.

If she worked a few more hours she could get back that £20 a week. Her friends were here and his friends were here. And this was Ealing. It was a nice place. A bit too much trouble round here sometimes, but it was not the kind of place that would ever see a riot (would it?).[14] The boy needed more, he needed something to do. He needed a dad.

'Mum, I'm bored,' he shouted from the living room.

What does everyone else do on a Saturday morning? she thought. What do they worry about, what will they do with their day?

'Mum, I've got nothing to do,' he complained.

'You need some exercise,' she said. 'Should be playing football.'

Maybe your dad would still be here if he'd exercised more, she thought; she never said it out loud. Maybe then they could have bought that flat. The home they really wanted, rather than be renting here. But she didn't say anything; she couldn't confide in the boy, could she? At this rate they'd be pushed out of London within a year.

She'd heard rumours the council were rehousing people out to the east, but soon they wouldn't be able to afford even that. It's not as if it was posh here, but it was home. They'd tease him about his accent if they moved north, or to Essex. What if they moved them somewhere where no one else was Asian? He'd get picked on. He was starting secondary school in two years' time.

West Ruislip to Northolt
All of these four families can sense how the social landscape tilts. None of these four families can see that landscape, but travel left to right, west to east, on the Central Line and at first you travel slowly downwards on one of the smoother slopes of what is in other

places a more wildly undulating invisible social topography.

We count distances in miles and kilometres, but in London, and especially underground,[15] more often distance is measured in seconds and minutes. We assess height as feet or metres above sea level, but in our great flat cities, especially today, elevation is more often measured in terms of enhanced life expectancy, inflated house prices or impressive school exam results. For every minute spent moving east past homes on the Central Line, the GCSE results of the children you pass by drop by four points. One grade C, worth 40 points, is lost every ten minutes on the tube while heading eastwards through this part of London.

Between the first four stations on the Central Line it is the accelerating drop in GCSE results that is most consistent. It is the sudden rise in poverty on entering Northolt that is most shocking. It is the relentless drop in average incomes that underpins this social landscape, the real landscape influencing people's lives: London pay not London clay.

The direction of the gradient on this part

of the line is about neither extreme riches nor dire poverty. This part of the line is typical of much of Britain. It is not that there are that many bankers to the west or that those bankers are not found to the east. It is that, at most, only around a single percentage of the population hereabouts work in well-paid jobs in finance. And, although life expectancy drops overall, the fall is not monotonic.[16]

Monotonic has two meanings. One describes the act of talking on and on in a monotone, a tone designed to ensure that boredom quickly sets in. Social statistics are often associated with monotonic lecturing. The other meaning describes a set of values that always go up or always down. Two of the five values shown below are monotonic, but only along just the first four stations of the line. These are GCSE results and household income. Both fall at every station as you begin to move east.

Five little charts,[17] each with four little bars, can sum up the first four stations of the Central Line: the general trend is downward in all these social measures, as you move from exurbia to suburbia. It's about schools, and avoiding 'bad

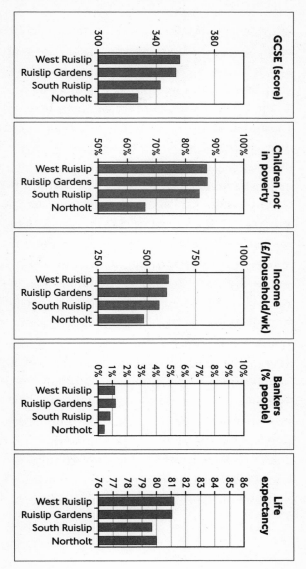

ones'. It's about money, and avoiding living next to the poor. It's about income, and keeping up appearances; it's *not* about bankers. It is about your health, but there is only a year's worth of life-expectancy difference between West Ruislip and Northolt. Then again, that makes over ten thousand years if you think of all the people who are losing out.

Ten thousand years is a hell of a lot. Just over ten thousand years ago and the last Ice Age was ending, the ice was melting, and the area that is now London was part of the Eurasian land mass, not on the edge of the sea. There was no English Channel, let alone Britain. Even if, in the grand scheme of things, each premature death might barely register, seen this way a year of life lost across ten thousand people is of geological *significance*. Seen from the point of view of a nine-year-old boy whose father is dead, it is more important than that. Life expectancy falls quickly when a few extra people die young.

Place matters and even what appear to be the smallest of changes between places matter. Later on along the line there are far greater shifts in life chances than are shown here, but few people cross over those chasms to move home from one area to the next.

It is along stretches of the line where conditions are more similar that people can envisage choosing between residential neighbourhoods, and so it is in parts of London like this where the local school exam results are so keenly observed, where housing prices and tenure exclude most of the poor from the neighbourhoods where chances might be a fraction better.

It is along the first part of the Central Line where household incomes drop so neatly in line with GCSE results, where few bankers live because these areas are mostly *beneath* them, but where people, on average, can expect to live around the national average length of life, if not a little longer – because here is better than average.

Greenford, 8.00 a.m.

'Have you seen my tie?' he asked.

'The wedding's not until 11.00,' she said.

He couldn't help it. He got up every day for

work during the week earlier than this, what was wrong with getting dressed now? Was it because the girl wouldn't be up yet?

'Where was she last night?' he asked.

'Out with friends. She was back at 9.00,' his wife replied.

'She's only twelve,' he said. He'd found the tie now and was a little happier.

'And her friends are only twelve and it was Friday night,' his wife pointed out.

'But where was she?' he said, shaping the knot to perfection. He liked everything to be neat. He liked order. He wasn't very good at talking to his daughter so he learned about her through his wife.

'She was at a friend's,' his wife replied. 'You look very nice. Why don't you wear the navy jacket with that?' she suggested, trying to change the subject.

'Which friend? They could all say they were at a friend's,' he retorted. 'There's been all that drinking on the recreation ground.'

'How would you know?' she asked, irritated. It was not as if he ever took much of a real interest in his daughter's friends, or in her friends, or in the neighbourhood. He'd been reading that *Greenford Green Neighbourhood News* on the toilet again, she thought. The four-page flyer had been sitting on the toilet for three months now. She wondered how many infections were passed on by junk mail that ended up as toilet reading matter.[18] 'Oh yes, the tie really goes with the beige,' she said, placating him.

Don't they realize how thin the wall is? thought their daughter. Mum's always telling him his ties are nice when they're rubbish. Ouch! Her head hurt. Most days she heard the two of them arguing about what he was going to wear. Not the stupid navy jacket, she thought. He thinks it makes him look young and 'with it'. But the beige one was worse. She winced. Maybe she should get an aspirin. That's what Mum does. She went to the bathroom. She had just managed to get the child-proof top off when her mum came in.

'Can't you knock?' she said.

'Don't let your dad see you with those,' Mum whispered. 'They're bad for you.

They're banned for children, even junior aspirin now.'

'But you take them, Mum, when you have a hangover,' she said, not too quietly.

'Shhh, he'll hit the roof. You shouldn't be drinking, not at all, and never enough to get a hangover, not at your age,' Mum whispered.

'I guess that's banned too?' she asked, a little quieter.

'Drink a pint of water, get in the shower, be good all day at the wedding and we won't say another word about it,' Mum pleaded.

'Can I have a drink at the wedding?' she bargained.

'Just a sip', said Mum. 'Your dad will get shit-faced and I'll be driving as usual . . .'

Perivale, 8.30 a.m.

He had thought it was funny when he was 13. They had erected a 'crime prevention marquee' at the tube station and one at his old primary school. They told everyone about the new infrared CCTV camera being put up on the cycle path, the camera that could see in the dark, the 'first of its sort to be installed in your borough.'[19] Now that he was 15 it was not so funny.

'This is a nice area,' his mum said. 'That's why we live here.'

'Yeah,' he muttered in reply.

'So why do some people have to spoil it all the time?' she continued. 'It will lower the tone of the neighbourhood. People will think we have problems here, they won't know how good the school is, and they'll see the signs and think we have problems. You know – problems.'

'Yeah,' he muttered, again.

'I blame the parents,' she said. 'Some of them aren't old enough to be parents. I was 38 when I had you. We saved up. You should have children only if and when you can afford them. That's the problem, all those young mums on benefit. It's their children and ones coming from outside the borough, that's why they've had to put the signs up, that's why the tone of the neighbourhood is going down.'

He glanced at the sign: 'Controlled Drinking Zone: It is an offence to drink alcohol in this controlled drinking zone if warned not to do

23

so by the police'.[20] His mum would kill him if she found out he'd been drinking in the zone. He and his mates had forgotten about the infrared CCTV, just for a few minutes. That was all it took. They only drank there because the signs were there, because it made them look tougher.

'It isn't illegal,' his friend had said. 'It means you can drink as long as the police don't ask you not to.' But he wasn't so sure. They had his face now, drinking, taken by that camera. He'd seen how it worked in the marquee. They store all the images forever on computer. They can see in the dark. They'd show his picture to the teachers at school. The teachers would identify him. The police would be at the door. He was already in trouble at school. What was the point? They had him trapped.

'I don't know why we came here,' she said, talking as much to herself as to him.

'Your dad works all hours to pay the mortgage. They're taking away your Child Benefit too – they say Dad earns too much. That's my gym money. Now they're talking about putting those high-speed trains though here. That'll hurt the house prices too. Thank God we don't live right by the line, but it will have an effect. Out at Ruislip they're campaigning for a tunnel, almost three miles' worth of tunnel! They'll get it too. No one will say, but it's because they're white out there, mostly white, not like us here. And look the other way, Hanger Lane's the same. We're squeezed in between. We might work hard, behave well, bring our children up right, but we won't get Child Benefit if they cut it like they say they will (Dad earns too much) and we won't get a tunnel, not through Perivale. Then we'll never be able to move out to Ruislip, no matter how hard your dad works, or how hard I work. I won't be able to go to the gym.

'You just see you work hard at school and don't get in any trouble.'

'Yeah,' he said.

Hanger Lane, 9.00 a.m.

'Hanger Hill ward is without doubt the most charming of all the wards in Ealing. It can boast of its wonderful parks, its golf course, its quality schools, its tree-lined streets and its

> thriving Conservative supporter base. Community
> involvement and participation is what Hanger Hill
> residents are all about. We welcome with open
> arms anyone wanting to help ensure that Hanger
> Hill ward is and remains at the top of the hill!'[21]

'Yuck,' she said, as she looked at the smug faces
of her two local councillors. 'Yuck, yuck, yuck,'
she repeated for effect. She was determined to
wind up her father this morning. 'Who delivers
these leaflets so early on a Saturday? They must
be paying them.'[22]

They were having breakfast in the conservatory:
marmalade on toast. She was embarking on
her favourite sport – goading Father. He was
studiously ignoring her. He was not going to
rise to the challenge, not when they had paid so
much for her education. It wasn't as if they had
relied on the state. That left more for everyone
else, didn't it, all those not at the 'top of the hill'?
And it was a hill, for God's sake, only a few could
be at the top of it. Why was she so ungrateful?
He pretended to be reading the paper.

'I wish we didn't live here,' she said,
determined to get a response.

'You won't have to soon, not if you pass your A-levels,' he replied coolly.

'I might defer for a year. I might live a little – you know, work, travel . . .' She was going to crack him, whatever it took.

'You can pay board and lodging,' he said calmly, his eyes moving across the type as if he were taking the words of the newspaper in.

'I'll leave and claim Housing Benefit,' she replied.

'No daughter of mine is claiming handouts while I'm alive!' he declared.

'I can do what I want now I'm eighteen,' she said deftly.

'Not under this roof you cannot,' he countered, 'and anyway, if you take a year out now it will cost you £27,000 to go to university.'[23]

'So?' she said. 'That will just mean I am not taking a handout.'

'It's not a handout!' he almost shouted. 'Your mother and I have paid all these years for your schooling. The least we should get in return is knowing you are not in crippling debt when you go to university. It's daylight robbery,' he announced.

'They are your yucky Tories who are charging £9,000 a year,' she said.

'Only because Labour wasted so much money on drop-in centres for druggies and Nelson Mandela buildings for other wasters, and anyway, when you go to university THIS YEAR, you will only have to pay £3,000!' he declared.

'I hate you!' she shouted, storming out.

'Why do you always rise to it?' her mother asked him later. 'She's just bored. There aren't enough other youngsters her age round here. People with children can't afford it.'

'They don't work hard enough,' he said.

North Acton, 9.30 a.m.

When was she going to grow up? her mother wondered.

'Haven't you got revision to do or something?' she said, pulling open the curtain.

Her daughter twisted her face into the pillow. She won a few more seconds of darkness.

'I'm not at school, Mum,' she complained.

Her mother retorted, 'You're twenty-one now.'

'I know,' she responded.

Her mother rearranged her argument: 'We only want what's best for you.'

The daughter negotiated: 'Exams aren't until after Easter. Don't worry. I'll have plenty of time to revise. I'm doing fine at uni. But there is more to life than just studying. Look, I'm saving money by staying at home. I've got the job in the bar to get the cash I need to buy my clothes. I'm very grateful to you and Dad, but I have to enjoy myself a little and the only time I can go out is after the bar closes. And there are night buses, so it's OK.'

'What time did you get in?' Her mother smelt a rat.

The daughter tried to explain: 'Oh, not too late, and it isn't as if there'll ever be any trouble here. If anything kicks off it will be in Ealing Green, down by the college, south of the main line.'[24] Skilfully she had changed the subject.

'Trouble, what trouble?' asked her mother.

'Kids. You know, kids with nothing to do. They're always hanging around down there.

Ones I used to know at college, the ones that didn't get to uni. They've got nothing to do.'

'They should get a job,' her mother retorted.

'There are no jobs,' replied her daughter. 'Anyway I'm at uni. Working at the bar isn't the only reason I have to get up. But what if I didn't have uni? What would I do? Work at a bar to pay the rent and to buy some clothes and then just sleep all day? What for?' She saw the older women's expression and stopped.

Her mother started: 'Before she had me, just before I was born, my mother was fighting for the right to work. Women weren't expected to work after having a child then. Gran was paid a pittance then, just because she was a woman. Women teachers got equal pay on my birthday. I bet they didn't teach you that at university! What about my jobs? Were none of them good enough? Not good enough because I didn't go to university? I didn't have a career because I had you! Twenty-nine was not young then. Not to have a baby. It was old. I wish I had gone to university.'

'You wish you hadn't had me,' the daughter said curtly.

'I didn't say that. It's just that most other mums round here seem to have more. I lost out. I'm doing a job you think even your friends who left college shouldn't touch. What for? To pay off the mortgage? By the time we do that you might have left home, if you ever find a job that is good enough for you!' her mother complained.

'I'm going to be a transport planner,' the daughter said. She knew her mother hated planners. They were going to turn Acton into the new King's Cross. This was her mother's favourite complaint: the building of that new 'Great Western Station' at Old Oak Common.[25] Planners would harm the value of the neighbourhood.

Greenford to North Acton

Within a year of these 16 people waking up along the westernmost extent of the Central Line the fears of the residents of Perivale came true:

> 'When Transport Secretary Justine Greening approved plans for the £32 billion HS2 link this month, she announced a 2.7-mile tunnel through Ruislip, in a concession to protesters who say their lives will be blighted by noise and disruption.

But their neighbours in Perivale and Greenford say they still face the prospect of 225mph trains thundering past their homes on the London-to-Birmingham route, as well as years of building work before its completion in 2026.'[26]

The four mothers we have just met, from Greenford through to North Acton, are unlikely to have to suffer much of the building work. Average-aged when they gave birth (for this end of the line), today they are aged 54, 53, 50 and 50.[27] Most will sell up and move further out of London before any disruption begins. That's what people of these ages tend to do in this part of the world. They are just waiting for their children to leave the nest. Their concern is for the equity they will lose in the value of their homes at the point of those future sales.

It's worth making a point about parents: these parents from Greenford to North Acton have all been quite old. From west to east these mothers were aged 42, 38, 32 and 29 when they gave birth. This is typical of north-west London: parents entering their sixth decade with children entering their second or third.

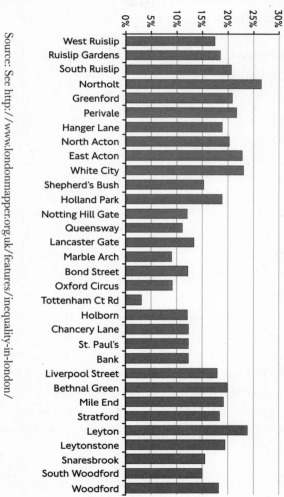

**Children aged under 16
(% of all residents)**

Source: See http://www.londonmapper.org.uk/features/inequality-in-london/

Their ages are taken from a nationally typical set of ages of mothers drawn from distributions revealed in recent official records.[28] In other words, for the places where they gave birth, in most cases for the first time, these mothers are not unusual.

The childhood demography of the Central Line is quite simple: two hills of relatively high numbers of children are separated by a valley of childlessness. The metaphorical river of never-growing-up is the one running down Tottenham Court Road. The peaks either side of the river of childlessness are to be found by Northolt to the west and Leyton to the east, places where just over and just under a quarter of all people are young children.[29]

East Acton, 10.00 a.m.

'It's only a ten-minute walk away,' he had said. She said she had brought him some new clothes so he could throw away the old ones. He liked to look smart. He'd always worried about how he looked. She had noticed it even when he was in playgroup. He had taken more care over his clothes than other kids had.

'It's only ten minutes back to East Acton,' he had said. It had been a long way for her to come, early in the morning, but she worked evenings. But this wasn't how she'd thought she'd be spending her Saturdays this spring.

When he was little she'd thought about how well he'd do at school, how he'd go to college, to university, meet a nice girl, get a good job, settle down, buy a house and make her a grandmother one day. Not too soon, mind, but one day. Now she was buying him clothes, and he was 24 years old. She remembered how she felt when he got out of nappies.

He was already reminiscing over her visit, which had just ended. 'It won't take you long to get home,' he had said. Had these been his last words? Why hadn't he said, 'Thank you for coming'? 'Thank you for the clothes'? Or just 'I'm sorry.' Was he sorry? It wasn't really his fault. He'd just been a bit slower than the rest. It didn't help that he'd gone to that school; that he'd not much liked his teachers. Maybe he'd been unlucky. But his mum just told him it was because he was slower that he kept on being the one that got caught. In here he wasn't slow. In here he was one of the quickest. In here he was one of the older ones at 24, not the baby any more. He wouldn't get caught so easily again. He didn't want his mum having to bring him second-hand jeans, again.

'It's only ten minutes.' That is what he'd said. But that was just the walk back to the tube. She had the time, she didn't have the money. It was the cost of the ticket that was the unspoken issue. The cost was £4.30, both there *and* back; £8.60 in all, or maybe £1.60 less with an off-peak day travel card.[30]

'You should get an Oyster card,' he'd told her. She didn't want an Oyster card. It would remind her. She didn't need it for anything other than visiting him.

'You'd save £4.60 if you got an Oyster card,' he'd said. 'It's just £2 on Saturdays.' She'd never had any kind of card, didn't want to get into debt.

'It's not a credit card,' he'd said. What did he know? She wasn't going to get in debt. She'd brought £10 in pound coins to spend on the two of them in the canteen. It had to be pound coins, she'd learned that. You can't take notes in.[31] But it hadn't been enough. It would be the only time she would eat out this week.

Altogether the tube tickets, the £10 of coins, the cheap charity-shop jeans came to more than £20. He'd be out in a few weeks, though. He thought he wouldn't get caught again, but he was the kind who always got caught.[32] He just got restless, and he wanted things, only good clothes, not second-hand jeans.

A minute later she was reminiscing over her visit. He hadn't even said thank you.

Visiting time for remand prisoners ends at 10 a.m. at Wormwood Scrubs on Saturdays.

White City, 10.30 a.m.

What was she going to do?

'Make it the history of the "now" of White City,' they'd said. 'Include a bit about the past but make it relevant to now.' She was googling 'White City'.

'BBC Breakfast's Sian Williams quits to escape move to Salford' was the headline in

37

Tuesday's *Evening Standard*.[33] Way down in the comments below the article she read:

> 'There seems to be a general assumption by many southerners that the BBC staff will have to uproot their families and live in Salford . . . so you're telling me that all the BBC staff live in White City? Most will aim for the wealthy Cheshire and Lancashire suburbs including Alderley Edge, Wilmslow, the Ribble Valley etc. and commute as they do now.'[34]

Well, she was BBC staff and she lived in White City, but only because she was 27, had not yet met the right person to settle down with and couldn't afford better. And, anyway, it was great when QPR weren't playing at home.

'The route of the Marathon in the Olympics in 1908' (she was googling again), 'went from Windsor Castle to White City.' But then she read that the last half-mile of the route was now all built over.[35] The year 1908 was too early for radio recordings or TV cameras and no good for reconstruction. And that date was no good. What she needed was an anniversary . . . She typed on.

'The Coronation Exhibition, 1911 . . .'[36] Now
she was on to something. 'The 22nd of June!'
she cried. Oh, God! That was too soon, she
couldn't make a programme in three months,
not even for radio, not from scratch. She read
more, faster, but she thought that 'George
Frederick Ernest Albert of the House of Saxe-
Coburg and Gotha', who became George V
that day, was hardly 'now'. The BBC didn't
welcome irony on how the royals were even
more Saxe-Coburg and Gotha than before,
ever since Liz had married Phil, who was
more German than Greek. But when had she
married him? When was Phil born? Who was
he? Why were his sisters not invited to the royal
wedding? Did the public really want to know?
Was there any anniversary in that? This just
wasn't going to work.

What's 'now', she thought? 'Politics' is now.
She shouldn't put single quotes around every
phrase. She thought harder. She thought,
right – why not the politics of 'White City'?
She hadn't bothered to vote last year; but
she could quickly find out who had, TGFG
('Thank God for Google').

She lived in Wormholt and White City ward. It took her a few more minutes to work that out – to work out where she lived! She ought to have known that voting was by ward. Well, she did now. Amazing what they didn't teach you at university.

'Good God,' she exclaimed. All three of her councillors were Labour.[37] Well, no wonder it's rough round here, she thought. You'd hardly expect Sian to live somewhere where almost everyone voted Labour. She'd heard that half the kids here were living in poverty, that it was worse here than the East End, but that couldn't be true, could it?

'Elections,' she said (to no one in particular). 'Damn.' None in 1911, but two in 1910; what was she going to do? And why was she working on a Saturday morning? She'd spent half an hour and just gone round in circles. Should she walk to work? The media village felt a bit like an open prison, all that security, with Starbucks outside for everyone to show off their new phones and pretend not to want to bump into anyone. Only the tragic people would be in on Saturday, she thought. And all the men were married.

Shepherd's Bush, 11.00 a.m.

He wasn't married, wasn't in a relationship. He was still in bed. He had a job but didn't work Saturdays and he had a hobby, the local history of Shepherd's Bush Green. It wasn't that he was a nerd. It wasn't that he had nothing else to do. It was just that what had happened round here in the past had been so fascinating, so important, and so few people knew about it.

Most people here didn't have kids. Kids were in White City or Holland Park. Here was just a bit too busy, a bit too noisy. But there was something else too. Here was where the poor were, and had been. The very poorest part was just north of here to be exact (and he did like to be exact), a place called Notting Dale. It was here, in 1911, that the highest death rate in London was recorded.[38]

The nascent Labour Party gained control of its first ward here, in 1906. In 1911 George Lansbury, the Labour MP, had published his pamphlet 'Smash up the Workhouse'. He read on his iPad: 'The Notting Dale Workhouse on

Mary Place was then renowned as "the cruellest in London".[39] The anarchists used to meet here and revolution was planned.[40] The American president had been shot by an anarchist just a few years earlier. The greatest abject poverty in London was found here on the way to Latimer Road, and 'the close proximity of one of His Majesty's Prisons for short-timers leads many of the prisoners, when they are released, to find their way here by sort of instinct' apparently, according to Robert Lee, a missionary writing on the area in 1902.[41] Just like my neighbour, he thought, out on bail from the Scrubs . . .

But then he read on:

'There is one feature of Notting Dale which strikes you forcibly if you go into a local crowd engaged in a heated argument, and that is the preponderance of the rural accent; for this is a district in which the evil of rural immigration has written itself large. Thousands of honest country folk crowd up year after year to the great city that they believe to be paved with gold. Of those who come in by the Great Western a large percentage drift to the Dale, failing to find room in the districts around the terminus; and in the Dale a process of moral deterioration goes on which is a tragedy.'[42]

Moral deterioration, just like his neighbours one the other side, then! His mind raced: except they're from rural Pakistan, not rural Padstow. He liked living here, he liked his neighbours despite their trading in illicit goods, and he liked making connections with the past.

He read out aloud the words of the Reverend Thomas Yeats, as spoken at the London City Mission's annual meeting held on 6 May 1911: 'Midway between Holland Park and Shepherd's Bush, with its western boundary abutting on to the White City, is the notorious district of Notting Dale, "that dark spot".'[43]

He turned back to read more of Robert Lee:

'Enquiring from old residents whether this part is better or worse than it was 10 or 20 years ago, I have received conflicting reports. For various reasons I cannot see how there can possibly be any change for the better.'

Robert Lee mentioned 'Freston Road', so he Googled it, and laughed to find what looked like

the offices of upmarket designer Cath Kidston
near this exact spot. It would be so easy to tell a
story of 'now and then', he thought. What has
stayed the same and what's changed, but would
anyone be interested? Any woman? He needed
to make himself more interesting to women.

Holland Park, 11.30 a.m.

'Is this how I'd expected to spend weekends this
spring?' she wondered, talking silently to the
baby in her tummy. She was 33 now; she'd be 34
when she gave birth.

'I'm 23 now, but will I live to see 24 . . .' she
sang. What was it with her and lyrics? They got
trapped in her head, but she was living about
as different a life from a Gangsta's Paradise as it
was possible to live.

'We spell it "Gangster" in Holland Park,'
she told the little one in her tummy. She was
just 16 when that song was number one. She
had always known she would go to university,
do well and marry well. No one who lived here
came from round here. If anything she was a bit

young to be a mum here at 33. She knew that –
for London – she was the typical age to be a
mother, but London was split apart, and the
chasms were widening. She'd read it in a book
on the tube. Nationally four out of ten mums
were older than her and five out of ten were
younger. She was the 'one in ten', the one in the
middle. Her dad used to sing that. She didn't
know where the song came from. She'd never
really known what that song was about.[44]

'Playgroup or nursery?' she asked the bump.
The schools round here were good apparently,
not just good but some of the best, but 'bump'
might do better in the independent sector.
They shouldn't put their principles before their
child's future, her husband always said. He was
in Manchester, away on work. He travelled a
lot. They'd thought of living near there briefly.
'Alderley Edge', 'Ribble Valley', everywhere
north sounded so rustic. At least everywhere
you might want to live. But his career meant
they had to be here. What if he had to find
another job? What of baby's future? Where
best to live to do well at school, go to college,
to university, to meet someone nice, get a good

job, settle down, buy a house and make her a grandmother one day?

She sang, to herself and the bump, 'I'm the child that never learns to read 'cause no one spared the time.'

There had once been a workhouse near here, she told the bump as she walked along Mary Place. She'd be pushing a pram along here soon. Was this where Mary Poppins was set, or was it Peter Pan? So many children's stories were set around here. Had the workhouse been Oliver Twist's? She turned left past Henry Dickens Court.

There are now places in Britain where, if you have a baby and it is a boy, he is more likely to go to prison than university; she remembered reading that somewhere too, her hand on her bump. But their mums weren't married, she thought. All the men round here were married. Her mobile rang and it was the father-to-be. He had something to tell her.

East Acton to Holland Park

Nowadays, in any typical week about one in 100 young men aged around 24 are being held in a British prison. That figure has risen since 2009, when it stood at around 0.7 per cent.[45] Part of the reason for the recent rise has been the arrests made after the riots of summer 2011, but also the provision of more space in prison for younger men, space made available due to that rioting.

Prison cells are a little like roads. Build them and they become full. A much higher proportion than 1 per cent of all young men have been in prison at some time during their still-short lives. At any one time the number of children who have a parent in prison in Britain is 160,000.[46] Estimates of how many children living in Britain will ever have had a father in prison during their school years have risen to stand at about 7 per cent,[47] the same percentage as go to private school. Britain sends more children to private school and more young adults to prison than do the citizens of any other country in Europe.

Along the Central Line the highest child poverty rate is found in White City: every second child there is poor. Poverty in White City means living on so little money that your income has to be made up by state benefits to be just enough money to survive. This is not to have enough to be able to hold your head up, to be respectable and to live at what most people would deem to be a minimum standard. That would require far higher pay and benefits.[48]

Most of the poorest children's parents are in work, and yet they are still poor. That poverty determines the nature of the home each child grows up in, exactly where that home is, what is in it and what is not. It is the tolerance of widespread poverty cheek by jowl with enormous wealth that underlies so many of the other divides in children's lives and life chances in a city like London.

Just two stops away, five minutes on the train, in Holland Park, are found the children who receive the highest GCSE results of anywhere along the line. Between Shepherd's Bush and Holland Park, two minutes' tube travel and a single stop, life expectancy rises by seven years![49] There are stretches of the line where the gaps between us are greatest. The eight minutes you travel from East Acton to Holland Park is a journey across a social chasm.

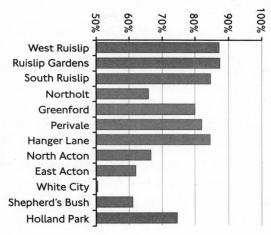

Children *not* in poverty

50% 60% 70% 80% 90% 100%

- West Ruislip
- Ruislip Gardens
- South Ruislip
- Northolt
- Greenford
- Perivale
- Hanger Lane
- North Acton
- East Acton
- White City
- Shepherd's Bush
- Holland Park

Source: See http://www.londonmapper.org.uk/features/inequality-in-london/

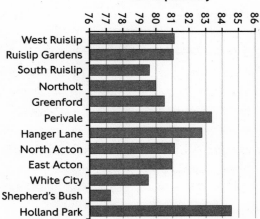

Life expectancy

76 77 78 79 80 81 82 83 84 85 86

- West Ruislip
- Ruislip Gardens
- South Ruislip
- Northolt
- Greenford
- Perivale
- Hanger Lane
- North Acton
- East Acton
- White City
- Shepherd's Bush
- Holland Park

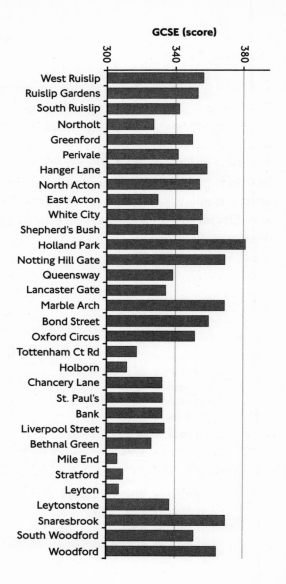

GCSE (score)

Source: See http://www.londonmapper.org.uk/features/inequality-in-london/

Notting Hill Gate, 12.00 noon

Noon on a Saturday was a good time for
canvassing. Not too early, just before lunch,
a good time to catch most people. It was the hour
they were often in, often up and often not eating.
He knew it didn't really make any difference,
but his local branch party were a bit shaken by
what was going on over towards Holland Park. It
was difficult to get good candidates there. There
were rumours. Ongoing revelations in the *Evening
Standard* did not help the party. What was it with
politicians, cheap thrills and pornography? [50]

Here, in Pembridge ward, Notting Hill *proper*,
as he liked to think of it, nothing untoward ever
happened. Just a few stops west, at White City,
and all the councillors were Labour. But that
was pinko BBC land. Here, all three councillors
were true-blue Tory. But here, as he repeatedly
told himself and his friends, was where the
wealth creators lived, not the leeches.

OK, so the house with the blue door that Hugh
Grant and Julia Roberts went in and out of was
in Colville ward, to the north, but that wasn't

proper Notting Hill.[51] It voted Liberal so it couldn't be![52] *Proper* Notting Hill was just south of where the annual Carnival route ran, between there and the tube station. That was Notting Hill *proper*. You wouldn't let the Carnival into Notting Hill *proper*. There was just too much valuable real estate. And the job of people like him was to protect property, to create wealth. After all, without wealth creators who would conjure up all the jobs? A friend had once asked him why there were not more jobs, as they were creating so much wealth? He told his friend that it was simple economics, but he didn't really have an answer other than that there were too many shirkers, leeches and troublemakers in the world. He just thought he was on the right side, he thought he wasn't a leech.

At 36 the local association considered him too young to be a councillor. Anywhere else in Britain and they would be begging him to stand, but here it was a privilege. This was the place to be, the place to be seen. If he turned heads here he could make it anywhere. This was where the movers and shakers hung out. Deliver a few hundred leaflets here, on a damp April morning, and you'll be noticed (they said).

Come to the cheese and wine parties, share
canapés with the great and the good. Princess
Diana used to jog round here. Palace Gardens,
the most expensive street in the world, was
just thirty yards across the Bayswater Road.
Helicopters land down there. They have private
security at the end of the road, men with
earpieces in. Here is where the money is.

'Good afternoon. I'm canvassing on behalf
of Kensington and Chelsea Conservative
Association. I wonder if we can rely on your
support in future elections?' he parroted cheerily
on her doorstep, his blue rosette on show.

'What elections?' she asked. 'You lot have
said there won't be any election until 2015. We
had the local election last year.'

'Well, err, can we rely on your support
for Boris?' he asked. He wasn't used to this.
Normally he spent a couple of minutes talking
about how terrible Labour was, but the mood
was changing, even round here.

'What about the libraries?' she asked bluntly.

He noticed she was not answering his
questions. 'We've got plans to save the libraries
and save a million pounds,' he said.[53]

She raised an eyebrow. 'Soup's on – got to go,' she said, shutting the door in his face.

Queensway, 12.30 p.m.

'You still look great,' he said. It wasn't the best thing to have said.

She enjoyed complaining about being 39, about being almost 40!

'It's not that bad,' he said. He was enjoying it, but it was OK for him. He was a man – what did he know? Even if he began to lose his looks he had everything else.

'For all you know you've got at least another 50 years to go,' he said, without thinking about it much.

He was practically spot on, she thought. She'd been looking it up, but then, he was good at estimating. That was his job, getting the guesses roughly right and sounding confident, but he wasn't doing a good job of charming her today.

'Look, love,' he said. 'You look great – you'll always be five years younger than me. We've got money. If you want a boob job for Christmas that's no problem. Let's just fit it in around the skiing.'

God, he didn't know her. He just thought everything could be bought. Holidays, happiness, her figure, it all had a price. People are so careless that they drive Porsches into the sides of houses round here.[54] Rolex watches and diamond rings are what you get mugged for here.

It's all about the money, she thought. It had been fun when she was younger, but everyone here was beautiful, and she *had* to stay beautiful. He *had* to stay rich. She hadn't had kids partly to preserve her figure, partly because he hadn't pressed. They could give money to charity instead, he had once joked. His firm gave a lot of money to charity. Lots of charity events to attend. All the women there seemed to stay the same age and weight. Were the men trading in the old ones for new ones?

'Where do you want to go tonight?' he asked. 'There's this exhibition on at the Serpentine Gallery,' he said, answering his own question. 'It's all about the tube. Different ways of drawing tube maps, and how it came to be built under the main roads, between the old estates. It was all about money really. The firm's sponsoring the show, free tickets,' he said. 'Good to show my face.'

He was looking down, scanning the paper, and not showing his face. It was all about pretending with him, she thought, all a show. The Serpentine Gallery was almost always free, but he wouldn't know, he didn't get out enough.

He got paid a huge salary for doing that job, let alone the bonuses. He wasn't a 'banker', he told her. Bankers live out of town or around Canary Wharf. He was an 'investor'. His fund invested; it didn't charge for services. That's why he could walk to work. Why he didn't have to work in a skyscraper. It was why his firm sponsored exhibitions at the Serpentine. Round here everyone who mattered could walk to work and also to everywhere else that mattered. It was odd that they took taxis or were driven so often.

He'd always liked maps, she thought. Maybe it was that geography degree he'd taken. He'd never been that good at numbers, or writing, or thinking really. Very sporty, though, had been in the first eleven at school and all that. Still watched the rugby religiously, but didn't manage to play as much as he'd like to.

However, he was a 'wealth creator'. So what did that make her? A 'wealth creator's girlfriend': she was too old to be a girlfriend. Thank goodness people said 'partner' nowadays, even people they knew. Well, she thought, so many well-off people were gay. Did gay people worry about growing old as much? Worry about being dumped for a younger model?

'OK, that's settled then. The Serpentine it is,' he said.

Lancaster Gate, 1.00 p.m.

Nothing was quite what it seemed around here. Everything was just a little skew-whiff. As if there had been a slight time-shift or something like that, as if all the signposts had been twisted somewhat just a bit to confuse the potential invading German parachutists and they had forgotten to put them back. For instance, here by Lancaster Gate tube, you'd think the people would be in Lancaster Gate ward, but they aren't, they're in Hyde Park ward; not that anyone lives in the park – it is a park! Most

people who live in Lancaster Gate ward take
the tube at Queensway, which is nearer.

He'd never understand the British. They
seemed to have no idea of their own geography
and they were always chiding him for how little
Americans like him supposedly knew about the
world. Being both rude and blasphemous when
telling him that war was God's way of teaching
Americans geography! They didn't even teach
geography properly here. It sometimes felt
like half the bankers he knew had degrees in
geography. What was that about? Was it some
old English class thing? Even Prince William,
'William Wales' as he liked to pretend he was
called (if only he were a US citizen), had a
degree in geography.[55]

He didn't get it, but then he didn't need to get
it. He wasn't staying here forever. It wasn't as
if he could ever afford to buy anywhere in this
town; well, not anywhere you'd actually want to
live. Anyway, work was helping pay the rent for a
little bit. 'Relocation', they called it. They could
take it off the firm's tax bill. And it wasn't cheap
rent – it was, literally, a daily hotel bill. This
country had all kinds of expense fiddles like that.

And no 'proper' free speech either; and a royal family. What century were they living in?

He was American, male, mixed ethnicity, an international accountant, aged 42, in Hyde Park, staying at the Sheraton, Knightsbridge, to be exact, and a bit lonely. That kind of summed him up. It was an amazing address. But the most amazing address was the one nearby. The one that confused plural and singular, advertising: 'One Hyde Park: The Residences at Mandarin Oriental, London, is the most exclusive address in the world; a residential scheme whose beauty, luxury and service place it in a class of its own on a global scale.'[56]

He was surrounded by wealth and he wasn't very wealthy. But there was something odd about One Hyde Park: too few people went in or out of the building. Maybe the people who owned the residences there were so rich that they chose never to visit them?

'Oh, to live like that,' he said, to no one in particular.

'But they must be lonely wherever they are,' he said, again to his imaginary companion.

'They can't really trust anyone when they have so much to lose.'

He wasn't badly off either, but here – surrounded by all this wealth – he might as well be a peasant. That's why they'd left England, some of his forefathers, all those years ago, to stop being peasants, and now he was back, in the heart of the new aristocracy. The flagship Rolex store (flashy wristwatches for those just begging to be mugged), McLaren retail (sports clothes for the unsporty to wear) – the old Mandarin Oriental Hotel (hints of opium wars and colonialism) and the new Bulgari Hotel (hints of Russian Mafia corruption). This was where it all came together, where all the money met up. Somebody had to count it in and out, and that somebody was him.[57]

Marble Arch, 1.30 p.m.

She was annoyed. Everyone made all these assumptions about her, just because she lived here. Even her family thought she must be doing all right: she had a job, she was a teacher and she lived in a 'Prospering Metropolitan

A' area.[58] Not bad for an Asian woman, but then there was that stereotype that she worked hard, and that her skin colour meant she was a Muslim. Well, she was a Buddhist. She was a mother. She wasn't rich and she lived here. She lived in Bryanston and Dorset Square; it said so on her polling card, but she lived at the north end of Balcombe Street, on the very edge of the ward. The place was only known, and not well known, for being where the Balcombe Street Siege had taken place, where the IRA bombers who had really bombed Guildford and Woolwich were arrested (the ones, it was rumoured, who were never actually charged). She knew all these things. Her neighbours didn't, or didn't care. She'd even added the name of the siege to the online Google map of the area. She looked out on to what had been mostly council blocks, looked on to Church Street, the next ward to the north: 'Inner City Multicultural' and lots of children. It was very different. She had more in common with the people there maybe.

'We're going out,' she said. 'We're going to the park. We'll go and see the Chinese boat on the lake.'

'Why do you like that boat?' her sister asked. 'What is it with you and boats?'

'I've always liked them, and anyway the park is free,' she replied.

'You'd have more money if you didn't live here,' her sister said.

'But I've always lived here. Why shouldn't I live here? I teach here,' she exclaimed.

'In a Catholic school and you're not a Catholic,' her sister teased.[59]

'I don't make an issue of it, and anyway the kids speak 36 languages there – how many of them do you think are really Catholic? The point is that they live here. I teach here. Why shouldn't I walk to work? Why should I live miles away?'

'Why do they live here?' her sister asked. 'Because the council flats are here, because their parents get their rent paid, like you?' This wasn't teasing any more.

'I don't get all my rent paid. If I got all my rent paid I'd be rich. And they all live here because they've got a right to live here, because here is their home too!' she retorted.

They were approaching the lake now. She always argued with her sister when her sister came to visit. She knew her sister didn't really mean it. She knew she secretly respected her for hanging on in there, for the results of the school, for keeping her politics true in a place like this. For being the one who walked to work, who talked about being green, who had a useful job, not just trying to make money, who had a faith and worked in a school with a different faith, and with people who assumed she was of a third faith, and worked out a way of living with it, but, for all that, her sister just couldn't stop herself having one last go at her 45-year-old younger sibling.

'But they only have a right to live here because they declare themselves homeless and with a connection to the City of Westminster!' she chided.

'Hardly any of them do that, and even if they did, what do you want to do about them? Make them live somewhere where there are no jobs, out of sight, on the edge of London, even further away? We have a map on the wall at school – I printed it off the Web. It colours places by how posh they are. Here, this ward, and just where the school is, is green – posh – but almost everywhere they come from, west and north, is red – poor. There's a lot of red on that map.'[60]

Notting Hill Gate to Marble Arch

You tend not to think of people living in the hearts of cities, but they do. Inner London has nothing like the urban population of a normal European city. Most people who work in the heart of London do not live in London. Over a million commute in each working day to areas where normally just a quarter of a million sleep. Even on a Saturday many come in for work, others to shop, sightsee, study or just stroll. In a normal large European city it is far more common to think of where you labour as also where you live. The closest-in many of us think of people actually living in London, regarding a part of London as home, is Notting Hill, the famously fashionable hang-out of the more affluent and, often, more svelte, younger businessperson.

In fact Notting Hill is slightly downmarket compared with the two stations either side of it. Life expectancy dips by almost two years in the minute it takes to travel here from Holland Park and it then rises by just over three years in the (officially timetabled) two minutes to Queensway. Queensway residents live longer than anywhere else on the line to average almost 86 years each. Who said inner-city living was harmful to your health? There are no guarantees that residents of the million-pound apartments in Queensway will live this long. For any individual, predicting longevity is prone to great error, but for groups of people the errors shrink.

Statistics are not certainties. Even for those clustered around each tube stop, a chance event, not looking before stepping on the zebra crossing, or that germ picked up from the cocktail party, can result in one fewer or one less premature death which is enough to slightly change the expectancy number for any given year. However, the overall shape of the panorama of the most important of life chances is pretty fixed over time, and it is shown in the chart of life expectancy (on page 129).

A slow rise to Perivale and then a much quicker descent to Shepherd's Bush, the cliff to climb to Holland Park and then the long descent from salubrious Queensway to stressful Holborn. A cliff face again, up into the City, the

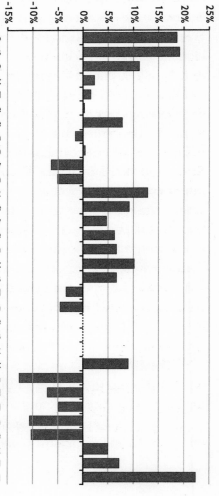

Tory less Labour vote (local elections)

West Ruislip	
Ruislip Gardens	
South Ruislip	
Northolt	
Greenford	
Perivale	
Hanger Lane	
North Acton	
East Acton	
White City	
Shepherd's Bush	
Holland Park	
Notting Hill Gate	
Queensway	
Lancaster Gate	
Marble Arch	
Bond Street	
Oxford Circus	
Tottenham Ct Rd	
Holborn	
Chancery Lane	
St. Paul's	
Bank	
Liverpool Street	
Bethnal Green	
Mile End	
Stratford	
Leyton	
Leytonstone	
Snaresbrook	
South Woodford	
Woodford	

fall to Leyton and the rise out north. Like an obstacle course. Vanatins in life expectancy are not unlike the pattern of voting (shown overleaf). Sometimes the slopes are a little less steep, but the cliffs are found in much the same places: between Shepherd's Bush and Holland Park, for instance, or just after Holborn, where people in three wards don't even get a conventional vote (in the ancient 'City of London'), or by the social cliff that has to be scaled when moving between Liverpool Street and Bethnal Green. Then, abruptly, just after Leytonstone the politics become very Tory again, despite the fact that people don't live as long. It is almost as if some believe that by voting that way they'll get the longevity that tends to be associated with such areas . . . But for now we are still travelling through those parts of the line where it is assumed that folk, most often, have it all.

Bond Street, 2.00 p.m.

At 2.00 on a Saturday it's just hell. Tourists! They are a curse sent to plague him. A curse for some great sin he had committed in a former life. At his time of life, at his station, he should be living out of town by now, but he needed to be around in case anything went wrong. And they had to do some operations on Saturdays. The human body didn't appear to appreciate the need for a day off shopping, or the Sabbath. What was even funnier was that they called this place 'the village', 'Marylebone Village'.[61]

Everyone associates Marylebone with a train station, not with one of London's premier urban niches. It was all the fault of that station on the Monopoly board game. It was even worse for Bond Street. Bond Street had to be posh: it was one of the green ones. Did Sotheby's locate their London offices on Bond Street after it had been coloured green or were their offices the reason for that colouring? Did he really care? That was just the kind of question they might come up with as part of the 'I'm so clever' consultants' Christmas pub quiz: all those new young registrars trying to show off, trying to get one up on their rivals. Well, he'd made it: 48 was still quite young to be a consultant specializing in cardiology. The fatter everyone got, the more work for him! It was just a pity that those getting the fattest usually couldn't afford to go private.

As he waited for her to return from the cloakroom in the little bistro they were eating in near Harley Street, it dawned on him that the real reason he lived in 'the village' wasn't the world-leading state hospital nearby and his NHS patients, but the work on the side, his independent consulting. The work that paid off the mortgage early, paid for the second home in France, paid for the skiing, paid for the lunch and dinners with the young female registrars (they always expected him to pay – so much for women's liberation). He had to be around, nearby, for popping in to give consultations in the evenings, on Saturdays, even Sundays. He worked hard. He should play hard too. The NHS work was really *philanthropy*; he sometimes told his much younger female companions this, when he'd had a bit too much to drink (at his private patients' expense). He was on the hamster wheel because the salary they pay in the NHS couldn't keep the wolf from the door.

'Jerry del Missier, the Co-CEO of Barclays Capital, got £47 million last year, almost twice what Bob Diamond got,' he had told her over lunch.[62] He'd 'read it in the *Daily Mail* so it must be true,' he told her, laughing at his own joke.[63] 'Do you know how many cardiac surgeons you get for £47 million?' It was a rhetorical question; she was just supposed to look interested and widen her eyes.[64]

'More than 500!' he exclaimed (he was using the old salary, for the basic NHS job, 9.00 to 5.00, few 'on calls', no London weighting, no out-of-hours work, no seniority awards or any clinical excellence awards, but he didn't want her to know about all those extras. She might start thinking he was greedy. He wanted to plead a bit of genteel poverty.

'If I just worked for the NHS I'd have to live miles away,' he explained. 'It is in the interest of my NHS patients that I also take on "independent" work so I can live nearby and also prep up on the very latest techniques. It's free training,' he said (he didn't like the phrase 'private medicine').

'Except they pay you,' she corrected him.

'Well, it is free training for my NHS patients

and I do a lot for the hospital charity,' he replied, paying for lunch (again).

She wondered if he thought of her as charity, whether he was really interested in her career and 'giving her some tips', or whether he just liked talking about himself and feeling hard done by. She hadn't gone into medicine to drink over lunch and then go operate on some rich private patient in a glorified hotel. She didn't envy him. She loathed him, but she needed his patronage.

Oxford Circus, 2.30 p.m.

The older woman was 51. This shouldn't be happening to her. She was too young. If it wasn't for the regular check-ups they would never have noticed. If it was not for the health insurance policy her firm took out on her behalf she would still be on some waiting list. If it took longer than 18 weeks to treat her at an NHS facility then, apparently, the NHS wouldn't worry how long it took as the hospital would have already missed its waiting-time target. The nice consultant had told her that. He worked mainly in the NHS, he had said. But there was a backlog there. That was why she was having her operation on a Saturday, and because she could be out and back at work for Monday morning.

It was just a minor operation, keyhole. They push a tube up one of your veins from your groin right up to near your heart and then put a little device in to widen the tube so the blood flows more easily. He'd shown her what it looked like on the screen. That was her heart, he'd said. 'Look. It has to work too hard.'

She'd always had to work too hard, and now she was lying on a trolley being moved from the ward to theatre to get her ready. 'Prepped', they called it. She'd be conscious throughout it, he had told her. 'Safer that way.'

She had everything. A Park Lane address. From where occasionally, with just one or two companions, she could pop into some of the finest restaurants in the land whenever she thought of doing it, or at least on weekdays, when they were not so busy. These restaurants were the kind where they brought your dinner in with a cover (cloche) over it and a waiter stood behind each diner to whisk the cover off simultaneously with all the other waiters. Had she eaten too much over the years?

She practically shared a back garden with Buckingham Palace, as she liked to say, exaggerating the geographical topology a little. She was valuable. Her firm needed her. They paid her enough, so she knew they valued her. And they needed her in on Monday. Was that fair? Shouldn't she get some time off? Her mind was racing. She was trying to think of anything but the operation, but the operation kept coming back into her head.

She was between husbands. It was the work hours mainly, that was why she hadn't had time to find the next one, and there was always so much to do around here. Everyone who was anyone had an apartment here. Rupert Murdoch had a place here. He stayed here whenever his London business was in trouble. She was surprised the paparazzi didn't film him coming and going; perhaps one day soon they would.[65] She guessed her tastes had become a little more expensive too, and all the older men seemed to have younger wives, of course. Round here the women did not look normal – all that plastic surgery (one day those boob jobs would come back to haunt them). But they were also selected for their looks. The young ones came from all around the world but had one thing in common – looks. The older ones had money.

This hospital looks like a hotel, she thought, as the trolley finally pulled into the operating theatre. There was her consultant:

'I'm just off to get gowned up,' he said reassuringly, as if he did this every day of the week. Was that a faint hint of wine she could smell on his breath? 'Nothing to worry about,' he flashed a smile back. His teeth were stained.

Tottenham Court Road, 3.00 p.m.

'The biggest footfall in Europe,' he said (trying not to sound like he'd said it a thousand times). He was talking about Oxford Street. They were walking from the tube towards the university campus.

'But cross the line, cross the street at Tottenham Court Road, and you are no longer in Westminster, you're in Camden,' he explained. 'It's very different.' He paused, then joked, 'It's not Kansas any more.'

She didn't enjoy the joke. She'd heard it too often, an occupational hazard of being called Dorothy.

'Still in posh south Camden mind, British Museum and all that, but 48 per cent black round here, out of 9,450 residents (although I'm not sure they got that number right),' and he reeled his statistics out: 'Estimated number of adult smokers: 1,990 to 2,530; estimated number of obese adults: 1,040 to 1,240; estimated number of adults binge-drinking: 2,070 to 2,610; estimated number of adults who eat five portions of fruit and vegetables a day: 4,140 to 4,210.'

He'd memorized those numbers well.[66] He was quite proud of his memory. It had helped him pass the 11-plus. That was why he was a lecturer, memory. Although now he was only employed part-time, a fact he tried to forget.

'How could they possibly estimate all that?' she demanded. 'How could they know the number of people who eat five portions of fruit and veg a day to the nearest 70 souls, or to the nearest 350 kumquats?'

She wasn't bad with numbers either. It crossed his mind that she might be taking the piss.

This part of London was like a chessboard. It is hard to explain if you can't see a map, but to go north-east you had to go east, then north-west, then east again. It was like tacking against the wind to sail a boat the way you wanted and the way the wind didn't want to go. He thought of trying to explain that to her.

'So where are all the smokers?' Dorothy asked. 'And how many were those numbers out of – 2,000 to 2,500 out of what?'

'Out of 9,450,' he said. 'Not many aged under 15,' he quickly added.

'So at least a quarter of adults round here are smokers?' Dorothy said, more as a disbelieving statement than a question.

'They could be. It's London, it's stressful,' he replied, a little hurt that she was not impressed by his ability to recall all those numbers. 'They're planning for there to be even fewer children here soon,' he said, trying to change the subject on to something he was surer of. 'There are 17 per cent drops forecast in under-fives in the next ten years, in Bloomsbury ward alone, 15 per cent drops in five to tens, 7 per cent drops in 11 to 15s,' he said authoritatively.[67]

'So they know how much sex we'll have then?' Dorothy was being more direct.

'No,' he said. 'They just extrapolate forward from the way things are going, and the way things are going there'll be far fewer children and more people our age here soon.'

'I'm not your age. You're 54,' Dorothy pointed out. 'And, anyway, young people can't get a mortgage now, so they have to stay around here when they get pregnant. There'll be more children, not less soon. Where do you get those numbers from? The banks could crash tomorrow. Who thinks they can forecast ten years ahead?'

Holborn, 3.30 p.m.

It was a lovely street, ever so quiet, pedestrianized, with the statue of a ballerina at one end. It was perfectly sited for the tube. Either Covent Garden (to get the tube to Heathrow) or Holborn, but quicker just to walk to Holborn to catch the Central Line, no point changing. She was learning that about London. It was often quicker to walk than catch the tube or even a taxi. One day she might master the bus map, but not yet. At her age, at 57, in a foreign country, that extra adaptation was a challenge too far. People expected you to be quick getting on buses and everyone was so fast around here. There were zebra crossings at the end of her street, but the taxi drivers appeared to resent you using them. And they talk about Greek drivers being bad!

When she had come here her nephew had given her lots of information about the area. He was a good boy. He was studying at the London School of Economics.

'The best in the world,' he always said. At least the high overseas fees were no problem for her family.

'It's the most expensive, so it must be best,' he had declared.

He was studying economics. She had asked him why it was better if it cost more. Surely things are better when cheaper? That is how her family had become rich. Buying cheap and selling dear.

'Cheap is best only up to a certain point,' he had told her. 'After that, when people are rich, expensive is better. Expensive watches rise in value as they age, but don't tell the time any better than cheap watches, less well as they age. These things are called Veblen goods.[68] The apartment you are buying near the Opera House is much smaller than cheaper ones you could buy just ten minutes' walk away, but its value will rise much faster despite that. It is because of where it is. It is because of the status it gives you. People don't go to the opera because they love the music. These people, the English, cannot even understand the words!'

Then, as she'd paid for the apartment in cash, he'd said, 'Anyway, you need to know where you are living. You'll fit right in here. Most people here live in apartments like yours; so many live on the fifth floor that it's almost like Athens. And most live alone,' he'd explained, handing her the printout he had brought.[69]

She didn't really want to live alone. She spent as much time away from the apartment as she could. It was nice when her nephew visited, but he would complete his studies soon and would be off to the USA to try his luck, with a little help from the family. He liked to pretend he was more American than Greek.

She knew her money was safer here than in Athens and safer in property than in a bank. She knew that if she returned to Athens for any longer than a few weeks at a time she might become liable for all the new taxes, and anyway Athens was becoming dangerous and depressing. But she didn't want to live alone and, so far, none of the other '54%' of people who were single (in Holborn and Covent Garden ward)[70] were interested in a 57-year-old Greek heiress.

She didn't like to let on about the money because she knew the kind of man that might attract. Already she had heard that Greeks like her (moving to London) were being called the 'new Arabs'.[71] Soon that label might stick, she thought. Should she pretend she was part American? Many British people didn't seem to like Americans either that much. She just didn't fit in very well. She was beginning to worry that it was not only her. Almost no one fitted in very well round here. They were all, in one way or another, here for the status. No one here belonged. Back in Greece she had been Greek. She was there because she was Greek and, if she was a little careful with how she talked and dressed, she fitted in well. Here, she was only here because she was rich.

Bond Street to Holborn

It takes exactly five minutes to travel these four stations. During those five minutes you pass under a greater volume of wealth than you can ever imagine possessing. You could put a value on the worth of this real estate, hundreds of billions of pounds, but that price waxes and wanes as the world's super-rich quickly turn from one safe haven for their often ill-gotten gains to another. What you can say is that you would be hard pressed to find another two or three square miles anywhere that were quite so pricey.

Directly above your head is Oxford Street and some of the most valuable retail property on the planet. Then, just a few hundred yards north and south of you, between Park Lane and Kingsway, between Green Park, Regent's Park and Hyde Park, is some of the most expensive commercial property in Europe, and yet tens of thousands of people also live here, often paying astronomical rents or holding astronomical fortunes in equity.

The living does not necessarily get easier as you move from west to east along this part of the line, even though you are moving nearer and nearer to the heart of the money, to the border of the actual City of London.

Life expectancy falls steeply from Bond Street to Holborn, by almost a year a minute. You never hear this statistic. The statistic of how, as you travel from the opulence of Grosvenor Square to the majesty of the Royal Opera House, with every minute travelled and every station passed a year of life is lost. Those kinds of statistics are reserved for journeys into the East End and yet, within the wealthy heart of London, there are gradients just as steep.[72]

For all his economist's training, our affluent Greek woman's nephew was not quite correct. His aunt would also need a society she could fit into, as well as somewhere her money would feel at home. Holborn is better suited to people of his age, a younger age. For her a better setting might have been a little further west, or it could have been a lot further west. The Dorset coast might have been a surer bet for convivial company for someone who was more afraid of being lonely than of being poor. For someone who liked being around children, who had none of her own, the heart of central London could be the very worst place to live, despite all her riches.

To travel from Bond Street to Holborn is to move towards a swiftly rising rock face. As you journey east, more and more of your neighbours are childless, young, and pay high rents, rents that use up most of their incomes. Those few who are elderly have less and less in common with the young. The loneliness may be harming their health. People from all around the world have moved here. All have not much in common except for now being Londoners. A Harley Street doctor, a City lawyer and a very affluent economic refugee are, in fact, all a little on the high income side for typical households along this part of the line. Only the ageing academic on his half-timer's salary fits the average; a great many are living on much less. Average incomes dip below £500 a week, less than £25,000 a year, where the Central Line crosses the Northern Line at Tottenham Court Road.

It is along this stretch of the line, in the shadow of the City, that the flotsam and jetsam of affluence are to be found. Here, even around Bond Street, the local Tory Party is trying to encourage new members to join. In an area of high population turnover its website insists: 'Our team reflects the diversity of our local community. There are people from six different countries among our younger and older members.'[73] Six is a remarkably low figure given the diversity all around them, but it is interesting that they mention it nevertheless.

Just five minutes to the east the same political party website (in April 2011) led with details of a fight for access to a Housing Association home: 'Labour Councillor Forces Young Family to Leave Home'.[74] It is worth noting how, by Bond Street and Oxford Circus, a majority of

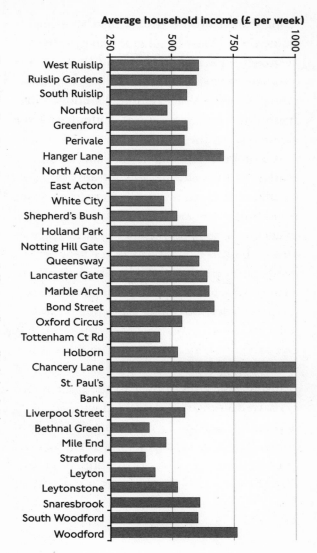

Average household income (£ per week)

Source: See http://www.londonmapper.org.uk/features/inequality-in-london/

local residents vote Conservative, whereas by Tottenham Court Road and Holborn, the vote is mainly for Labour.

There is a fault line running through this part of the heart of London. A fault line that has grown more perilous in recent decades as the people on the ground either side of the line have been pushing in opposing directions. When a riot occurs, when protesters occupy shops, when there is trouble in town, the social earthquake now more often than not finds one of its foci near here. But, just like earthquakes, although *where* trouble occurs tends to be predictable, precisely *when* trouble will next occur – when the tension will next cause the ground to shift – nobody knows.

Chancery Lane, 4.00 p.m.

'It's funny,' he said as they came out of the tube. 'Although Chancery Lane is the boundary of the City, this tube stop, the one given its name, is outside the old walls. It's not easy to spot the point where you cross over from the

Borough of Camden. You wouldn't know you are in "the City" unless you looked carefully for the signs, the livery, and the street furniture changing. Cross this line,' he said, making a point of stepping theatrically over the kerb as they entered Furnival Street from the north, 'and you leave democracy and enter another place. We don't get to vote here. There is no MP for us residents of the City of London.' They walked past three security cameras on a pole in the street and the older man gestured towards them as if this were further proof. His younger companion was interested, but not that interested.

'My part of the old City is called Farringdon Without, or it could be a detached part of Farringdon Within,' he pontificated. 'Someone moved the boundaries about ten years ago. I've never really got to the bottom of it; anyway here we are. And . . . this is where I live,' he announced, opening the door for the man he had chatted up over lunch.

He still looked good at 60, kept himself fit, probably fitter than the younger man. Maybe it was because he was black that people found it hard to gauge his age; most assumed he was in his forties. They often didn't guess that by shaving his head he disguised how little hair he had left.

'What do you mean you *leave* democracy?' the younger man asked.

It was just dawning on him that this was the flat of someone a little older and a lot more prosperous than he had assumed from their chat in the wine bar. Was it because the older man wasn't white that he had judged the chap to be a social class below the one he clearly was so solidly in? This was a no-expense-spared apartment.

'The City of London: a unique authority,' the older man quoted. 'That's what it says on our website.[75] What that means, what's unique, is that people here do not get to vote for who represents them. But what is really funny is that we pretend they do. My job is to work as a kind of public relations officer for the City. We call the men with power "councillors", but they are not voted into office like other councillors. We call our sheriffs "elected", but we don't say who gets to elect them. It's really a benign dictatorship here. But it works. No one complains. There is just so much money within and most people outside just don't know that government here is less democratic than almost anywhere else in Europe.'[76]

'So why are you here, then? Surely you don't fit in,' the younger man asked, a bit abruptly. What he really wanted to ask was why hadn't he let on that he was loaded a little earlier?

'They need me,' the older man replied. 'I help them feel less guilty. Secretly they are feeling more and more guilt with every year that passes. People used to be impressed by them, but that is going. Now they are becoming the bogeymen – old white unelected bigots who order in their private police force to attack legitimate protesters, all that kind of thing. They need diversions. I'm one of their diversions: I'm what they call their "corporate responsibility". I show they care, but – to be honest – they don't really give a damn.'[77]

'So why are you helping them?' the young man asked, a bit more unsure again of his new companion.

'I get the flat,' was the simple reply. 'You don't think I own this place, do you? It comes

with the job. I get to live in London town. I get
to be at the heart of it all. I'll get a pension –'
he saw the younger man's eyebrows rise and
wished he hadn't mentioned the pension – 'and
maybe one day I'll write a book about all the
corruption and hypocrisy that go on here, from
another country, somewhere warmer.'

His younger companion looked more
impressed. A pity he'd signed that non-disclosure
agreement: it read like the Official Secrets Act.
Would they stop his pension if he wrote that
book?

St Paul's, 4.30 p.m.

She always did well outside the cathedral. They
charged so much for people to go in that a few
pennies for an old woman with a shopping
basket on wheels was not going to hurt.

She looked much older than her 63 years,
more haggard. That was hardly surprising.
If she got enough from begging she could
pay to stay in the 'youth' hostel. At 63 and as
'vulnerable', she had a right to be housed by

the council, but she was frightened of the estate they would put her on.

She was here at 4.30 because she didn't have enough for the hostel. The hostel would have let her in at 2.00, but she didn't have the money. She would almost certainly be sleeping in the shelter tonight and it opened much later. She liked it in the hostel, all the young people around. If she didn't get another few pounds she would have to go to the shelter, which wasn't as nice. But then people didn't think she was nice. If the youth hostel was booked up she'd have to sleep in the shelter even if she got enough money. It was so confusing. She got confused a lot, repeated herself a lot. But her long-term memory was good, even her memory from a few weeks ago was good. It was just having a conversation and remembering what she had to do today that she found hard.

For example, she'd been begging here exactly a month ago. She thought she'd been asked if she could move on by a BBC camera crew, but she hadn't been. They had said something about filming for the 300th anniversary of the building of the cathedral, about how

£40 million had recently been spent smartening it up, about how it was 'now looking certainly as clean and as brilliant as it was 300 years ago when Christopher Wren built it'.[78] They sounded as if they were reading out a script.

She wondered if they had made people like her move away back then, so as not to spoil how the building looked. She guessed they had. Some things do change, but people never complain enough, she thought.

Different people treated her in different ways. The haughty grumpy old ladies who volunteered to police the tourists within St Paul's tended to look as if they were holding their noses as they walked past her. This was when she was having a rest by the side entrance.

'Not very Christian,' she would mutter, but then this wasn't really a very Christian building, it was a tourist attraction and maybe something a bit worse than that, she thought. Once, early in the morning when it was quite empty, one of the younger security guards had asked her if she'd ever been inside. She'd said she hadn't. He had told her that he spent hours sitting high up in the dome, making sure tourists walked round the right way. He'd taken her in to see the inside for a few minutes, before the haughty ladies arrived. It was full of statues of dead soldiers and their horses, of admirals and generals, of people who had started wars and killed thousands.

'What's this got to do with God?' she'd asked.

'Search me,' he'd said. 'But sitting up there eight hours a day pays my rent and pays for the Oyster card – if little else. I meditate sometimes and think about Allah.' He was laughing, as he carried on: 'Everyone's here for the money: you begging, me sitting, the tourists buying their experiences, the clergy selling peace-of-mind to sinners.'

Last Tuesday she was sitting outside and saw someone she recognized coming in, a woman who had been a Member of Parliament when she was a teenager, Shirley Williams. She asked Shirley what was happening.

'We're debating the Robin Hood Tax,' the former MP answered.

'What good will that do?' she asked Shirley. 'All that debate, it doesn't change anything. No one will take any notice. You want to make more of a fuss. That's what your mum did. She

wrote a book, didn't she, against war, against
all that this place stands for? She made a fuss.
That's how we got the NHS and everything:
making a fuss. If you don't make a fuss we'll
lose it all!'

The former MP walked off wondering
why so many very elderly people appeared to
remember her best for her mother's book, not
for the Social Democrats.[79]

Bank, 5.00 p.m.

'I don't know what they are complaining about!'
he exclaimed. 'I'm 66 and I have years of energy
left in me. People should only retire when they can
afford to, when they have saved enough. All these
namby-pamby shirkers wanting to stop working at
60 and take those government pensions that my
taxes pay for, it has to be stopped!'

He was on a roll. She tried to get him off it.

'But you are unusual, dear. You've always
had so much energy and drive. Some people
just want a rest by their seventh decade, to slow
down a bit.' She was thinking wistfully of their

94

home on the Med near Nice. It was always so warm there. People were so much calmer; she could see why they lived longer in France. She had failed to change the subject. She should have mentioned more details about how good, how hard-working he was. She poured the tea. They always had tea at 5.00 on Saturdays. Always left it to brew for the correct amount of time and always put the milk in afterwards.[80]

'Is it because our china dates from the nineteenth century that it is safe to put the milk in afterwards?' she asked, successfully deflecting his attention on to his enormous knowledge of antique porcelain trivia and his constant need to show off.

'From the 1760s I think you'll find,' he said. And then he spoke of what happened to be on his mind at that time and she just had to catch on '. . . and did you know that the Central Line at Bank station curves so sharply that if you stand at one end of the platform you cannot see someone standing at the far end? Always a bit dangerous in case a chap should be thinking of jumping!' he added, a little tastelessly, quickly correcting himself with a further dose of trivia.

'It is all because of the land ownership above the line,' he said. 'The company involved, a private company mind, was allowed to build the Central Line beneath the streets for free. They especially wanted to avoid heading anywhere like here. Our ward, Queenhithe, is a residential ward, you know. Very complex land rights. It all dates back to the Roman dock –' He was just getting in his stride and was about to lecture her further.[81]

'But the Central Line runs north of St Paul's Cathedral,' she said. She was very thankful she had got him off the subject of other people being shirkers, but she really didn't want to get on to his favorite topic: the City and its place in the ancient order of things. 'It's the Circle Line that runs under us,' she explained.

'And Waterloo and City,' he interjected, not wanting to be outdone on the tube trivia. 'And the Northern Line is just a few hundred yards away.'

'I wish we could have been at the Stables this weekend,' she said, to score a point for future use and move the subject on.

The Stables was their third home, just

south of Guildford, where the land was a little cheaper (he had said). It was where they could keep the horses, so they called it the Stables; they had five bedrooms there too.

'I know,' he said, although he didn't really like weekends out there, not if they didn't have company. 'But we have to be in the City for the function tonight. That charity bash – you know, about providing more homeless shelters in the East End, so people can't hang about here messing up the streets. It is just too bad for business. It loses the country money.'

'As much as us claiming our first home is the apartment in Nice and registering as non-doms for taxation?' she asked pointedly, thinking that a more direct rebuttal might be more effective this time.

He ignored her, hoping she wasn't passing through a 'red phase' like their daughter, brainwashed by all those Marxists. He read aloud the first line of the speech he had prepared for this evening's dinner: 'The harm being done to the City's reputation by the unsightly mess is considerable.'[82]

Liverpool Street, 5.30 p.m.

'Ninety per cent of you are fucking illegal,' was
that what she had heard the man saying on the
tube? 'I used to live in England, now I live in
the United Nations,' he'd said.

She had sat there quietly.[83] The Asian men
were going to answer him back.

'We're British. Watch what you say – keep
yourself to yourself,' they had shouted in return.

It wasn't looking good. She had been glad to
get off.

'As long as you're fucking working and not
claiming benefits,' was the last thing she heard the
racist shout. It took so little time, she thought. So
little time from a politician saying something to it
being shouted by some drunk thug on the tube.

'I pay more taxes than you do,' one of the
Asian men had replied.

It was sad, she thought, that he was speaking
the same language really, saying he had rights
because he had a job and paid taxes, not just
because he had rights whatever work he did.
But then, she didn't pay taxes, not any more.

She didn't work, not now she was retired, now she was just a year short of her three score and ten.

Liverpool Street was the nearest tube to her flat, but often she stayed on until Bethnal Green and walked back. It was a bit further, but she didn't really like all the bustle of the mainline station, or those young people, all the women and men in flash suits, all the shiny tall buildings. It only took a few minutes to clear them, but somehow she felt better walking back from Bethnal Green, though the Green wasn't like it used to be either.

She'd grown up in Spitalfields, was born during the war, in early 1942, when everyone thought they were going to lose. She'd been too young to be evacuated. Now they called the place she lived Banglatown.

Liverpool Street had been taken over by posh young bankers; Spitalfields by Bangladeshis moving in from Sylhet. She preferred them to the bankers, but she didn't like how everything was changing so fast.

Her family had come from Ireland, her grandad had come for work. The area had all been Jewish then; he'd told her this when she was a girl. It was like a ghetto, he had said. Like that ghetto in Warsaw.

She had been friendly with a Jewish boy, but his family moved to north London. All the Jews had moved out; a lot of the Irish now too. She thought that it wasn't so much a 'United Nations' as a set of refugee nations now. Not that the Bangladeshis had been refugees. They'd been British when they first came over. It was the British that had stopped them being British.

She laughed to herself. Her grandad had always laughed at the British. She'd always remembered that when the National Front was marching round here, when she'd had her kids, in the 1970s. She'd never been tempted to support them. They were long gone now – her kids, not the NF, who were back. They – both her kids and the NF, who were now called the BNP – told her she should get out too, but she'd always lived here and, anyway, this was where her tenancy was.

The council was making noises about wanting the flats, something to do with refurbishing the building as a homeless hostel. Money was being donated by City bankers, they said. She didn't care. Why did they have to have her home? They said she had too many bedrooms, because she had one spare and the one she slept in.

Chancery Lane to Liverpool Street

The six-minute journey from Chancery Lane to Liverpool Street station takes you, underground, from one boundary of the City of London to the other. The City of London Corporation has been described as 'the nation's last rotten borough, in which ballots in 21 of its 25 wards are controlled by companies, whose bosses appoint the voters'.[84] Within the City, statistics on the characteristics of local residents are harder to obtain than is the case outside.

Unsurprisingly the very highest average incomes along the whole of the Central Line are recorded by people living along this part of the line, but there are also others eking out an existence on a tiny fraction of those sums.

Gratifyingly, given the station's name, the 2001 census revealed that the highest proportion

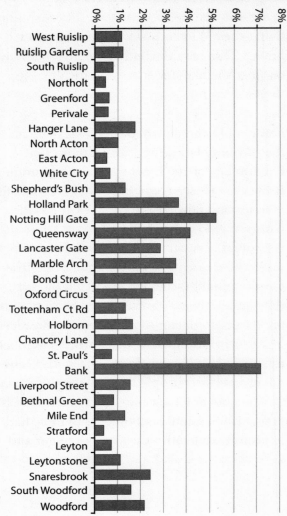

Bankers (all residents working in banking)

Source: See http://www.londonmapper.org.uk/features/inequality-in-london/

of bankers were found to be living in the two wards that are closest to the Bank tube station. The second highest proportion (and a far greater absolute number) were found living west around Notting Hill.

Since 2001 the City of London has risen up even higher in terms of new buildings, new people and new wealth. It was here, in the Mansion House, that those successive Chancellors of the Exchequer, from Gordon Brown to George Osborne, bowed down before men like the 66-year-old banker whose wife wished she was elsewhere.

When the crash came the banks were saved. But the cuts to public services and the Corporation Tax cuts for the rich mean that the City will continue to feel a need to 'support good causes' for some time to come. However, it is unlikely to support 'charity' quite as much as before. Not if it has to trim its own excesses a little.

The man at Chancery Lane may find he is taking his pension a little earlier than he had expected, while others who are younger and poorer will have to take theirs much later in life, or will die before they can.

Life in the months after April 2011 changed most for the woman who used to beg around the cathedral. Her pitch became a city of tents. Suddenly, for a few months, she was no longer so unusual, but when she tried to beg again at the end of February, after the tents had gone, she found she was quickly moved away by the new security guards who were even more watchful for anyone trying to pitch up.

The homeless woman would die soon after, and her death would be followed shortly by that of the woman who had behaved well all her life, but was living in a flat with one too many bedrooms and who took the pills because she couldn't face leaving her home.

Bethnal Green, 6.00 p.m.

'What do you mean you're not too old to have a baby?!' she shouted at her daughter. 'You're almost 50. You have two children. What do you want another one for? I had you when I was 23. That was a respectable age to become a mother! That was a good age for you too, wasn't it? But you should have stayed with that man. He was not a bad man!'

'But I didn't love him, Mum,' her daughter responded.

'So what? I didn't love your father,' the 72-year-old grandmother-to-be replied.

'Yeah, but your marriage was arranged. You didn't expect to love him,' came the reply the older woman had heard too often before.

'That's how marriages were then. Things were simpler then. We didn't have much but we didn't want for much. Now they say half the children round here are poor and the other half might as well be.[85] But it's a different kind of poverty to the one I grew up with. We thought everyone in Britain was rich. When we got here we got a shock, but it was nothing like Germany. Do you know what I first remember, from during the war?'

She had begun telling her story again. Her daughter *had* to stop her.

'Mum, I've heard it all before. You were Kindertransport, except you can't have been, that was for children just before the war. They call them unaccompanied asylum seekers nowadays. They're trying to make sure none of them get locked up in detention centres,' her daughter gabbled on, attempting to change the subject.

Her mother always warmed to darker subjects. Her mother was not to be silenced.

'Round here, after the war, things changed. The new prime minister, he was MP for Limehouse, you know, he made sure we got things – got doctors for free, got spectacles, got food. It was rationed all the time I was growing up, which was great, as the ration for children was large. We didn't go hungry, and by the time I married your father there was work for everyone, and new homes. They were building more homes then than they'd ever built . . .'

Her mother could have carried on and on. Her daughter interrupted.

'Yeah, but look at the place now. Who stayed? There's only you here now, everyone else is an immigrant. And look at the blocks now, finally they are having a makeover, finally something is being done about the kitchens, finally PVC window frames are being put in. But this block is 60 years old. Who wants to live round here now?'

Her daughter was sick of hearing about how good the good old times were. She thought of saying that the new windows should be double-glazed too, but she didn't want to rub it in.

'But I'm an immigrant,' her mother replied. 'This is where I belong.'

Mile End, 6.30 p.m.

They'd always lived here, generations of them. They had an Irish name, but that practically made them cockneys. He'd been born at the worst time, 1937. Amazingly he was still alive. Maybe it was something in the water – or something *not* in the water any more. This was his joke. They didn't get it, the youngsters, didn't know that water hadn't always been piped, didn't know what *potable* water meant, but then there was a lot they didn't know.

It was the schools here. Everyone said they were bad,[86] but generation after generation of his family had gone to the same ones. And the next generation would too. The next generation was coming. His grandson (or was it his great-grandson?) was 19 years old and had just become a dad.

When he was 19 it had been military service and he would have been shot had he gotten a girl pregnant, or there'd have been a shotgun wedding. People had different values then. Everything was a bit simpler, he thought.

Now there was the college. Queen Mary 'University', they called it. He could remember when it started to be built on the bomb sites and then expanded and expanded. But it was only recently that it had got so huge. It was funny, he thought, funny that there was an enormous university here, but that the kids who went to school here still didn't pass their exams. He guessed some must have passed, but people didn't seem to want to live here unless they were students or had no choice or both. Funny, that.

Mile End was so near to the City and to Canary Wharf. He couldn't really work out what it was. What were they afraid of? Was it the schools? Was it all the immigrants? There was something about Mile End. Even his own children had left the area (those that could), moved out to bigger homes in Essex.

It was the younger generations that remained until they made good. The phone rang. It would be his son. He always called at 6.40 on a Saturday. Just after *You've Been Framed* (on ITV) and just before *Dad's Army* (on BBC). It was the immigrants, he thought. No immigrants in *Dad's Army*.

Stratford, 7.00 p.m.

She liked *Dad's Army*. Must have seen it hundreds of times. It reminded her of the past. All the family had watched it when it was first on; that would have been in the 1960s. It wasn't that she found it funny. It was just that it reminded her of that time, of when they were young, of when the children were young, and of something else, of a different way of living. It was hard for her to put her finger on it.

People round here had never had much. She'd heard wages were the lowest in London.[87] The Olympic Park would change all that.

Ken Livingstone had said, in his speech just after they'd won the competition to host the Olympics. He said that he had only bid for the Olympics to try to finally get some decent money into the East End.

She could remember when there had been more money about, when everyone who wanted a job had one. Her great-granddaughter had never had a job. The youngster was 23 years old now and pregnant, so she'd become one of those 'benefit scroungers', the ones that they were always going on about in the papers.

'Benefit scroungers' sounded like a new phrase; but she thought she'd heard something like it before.[88] When she herself was 23, back in 1957, the Prime Minister, Harold Macmillan, had told them they 'had never had it so good'. But she thought they had it better a few years later, better when they took more of the cash off him and his lot.

She'd always been interested in politics. Her mum had told her what it felt like not to be allowed to vote. And she'd always voted, but something big had changed during the course of her life. She'd noticed it first when she was

43, in 1977, during the Silver Jubilee. That was when the National Front had started acting up around here. Maggie Thatcher had said much the same things as the NF, but in received pronunciation and while wearing pearls. And then Maggie had cut taxes for the rich, and Labour had not reversed that. That was why she'd grown to be suspicious of them all.

She was worried for her great-granddaughter and the new one to come. Herself, she'd lived a good life. She was 78 this year. That's as long as most people got to live around here.[89] People round here were always getting taken for a ride, by the NF, by Maggie, by Labour (when it didn't really care), by the BNP.

She's heard that some 15 years ago, in 1997, when that Tony Blair had come to power, three-quarters of the richest people in Britain were rich because of old money, money they had inherited, money that her people had failed to take off them. But now three-quarters of the richest people in Britain were rich because of money they had made.[90] That is money *they* had taken off people like *her*. No wonder wages here were so low, and *falling*.

Using the word 'creator' from the Bible, they called themselves 'wealth creators', but they took the wealth away from most people. The new baby, her great-great-granddaughter, would not even qualify for the Labour government's meagre Child Trust Fund. That was to be cut.

They said they were 'job creators' too, but ever since they had started taking so much of the wealth once more, the jobs had begun to dry up.

She wished she had someone to talk to again, but since her husband had died she'd had to start talking to herself a little more. *Dad's Army* had finished. It was time to do the washing-up.

Leyton, 7.30 p.m.

More of her friends were dead than alive, but 81 was a good age to get to. Her granddaughter had told her, 'Round here people live some of the shortest lives in London.' That had not been very tactful, she thought, but it had been nice to see her again. She was at university now, a 'mature student'. It was funny they called her mature at 25. She was doing a 'dissertation', she'd said. Such long words they used now. Queen Mary and Westfield it was called,[91] the university her granddaughter went to, that is.

'They only let me in because I was local, Gran,' she'd said. 'Something about "widening participation", but that's all ending now.' Her granddaughter was the first to go to university in the family. She was ever so proud of her. But her great-granddaughter might not go '*apparently*' (another word the youngster had not used before she'd gone to '*uni*').

The youngster read posh books now. In one it said that in the hour it took to go on the Central Line from its furthest point west to Leyton, on average you would have lost nearly ten years of life expectancy. She didn't quite understand what 'on average' meant, or how you could lose years of life just by moving east, but '*apparently*' you could.

'Gran,' she'd said, 'I need to interview you for my dissertation. You've got to read what it says here about where you live – I got it off Wikipedia – and then I want to know what you think about it.'

She still had the piece of paper:

'It is a very diverse, ethnically mixed ward. Sixty-three per cent of Leyton's residents come from a Black or Minority Ethnic (BME) community – mostly from the African-Caribbean and Pakistani communities. Since May 2004, however, when the European Union expanded to take in twelve new countries, there has been a rise in the number of Eastern European people coming to live in Leyton. Many have settled there to work, study and start a new life.

Leyton is a very deprived ward. It has the highest rate of teenage pregnancy in Waltham Forest, the highest rate of unemployment, the highest percentage of pupils receiving free school meals, and the Beaumont Road estate – in the north of the ward – has been assessed as the fifth most deprived estate in Britain. Alongside two other large estates – the Oliver Close and the Leyton Grange – the existence of the Beaumont also makes Leyton the most densely populated ward in Waltham Forest. Some estimates are that up to forty per cent of residents are living in overcrowded conditions.

Despite the many serious challenges it faces, Leyton has a vibrant community and a lot of hope. Half of the ward's population is less than thirty years old.'[92]

She hadn't really known what to say to that. Then, '*Actually* . . .' she began to explain to her granddaughter how it really was and why it really was . . .

Bethnal Green to Leyton

The couple talking in Bethnal Green were not typical. It is not just that very few older Jewish people still live there but that, for the daughter, 50 years old is unusual to be pregnant, although it is becoming less unusual. There are more children in the East End than in the centre of London, but – it may surprise you to hear – not quite as many are alongside this tube line as it runs through the West End of London.

What is more *usual* along this part of the line is to have children earlier and for generations to be more compact. It is grandchildren and great-grandchildren who have been becoming parents at 19, 23, 25 and, a little further east, at 28 between Mile End and Leytonstone (inclusive).

Along this section of the line the residents have not been typical of much of the population, but then most people are in some ways not typical of most of those who live around them. Here it has been the old age of the people (whose half-hours we have invaded) that has made them stand out. By the time we get to Leyton we have met the first person who has lived for longer than most people around her ever get to live. This will continue as we move north-east, as, although life expectancy jumps up with each of the next three tube stops, it doesn't rise as fast as the extra three years of life between each person we will visit. However, despite this rapid ageing, the next few residents will become more typical again, as far higher numbers of older people are found in outer London than inner.

What does stand out about this part of the line is how, along the long course of four widely spaced tube stops, between 40 per cent and almost half of all children are growing up in poverty. Entire families in block after block are living in poverty and many of the elderly will be poor too. Here it is not like the encircled White

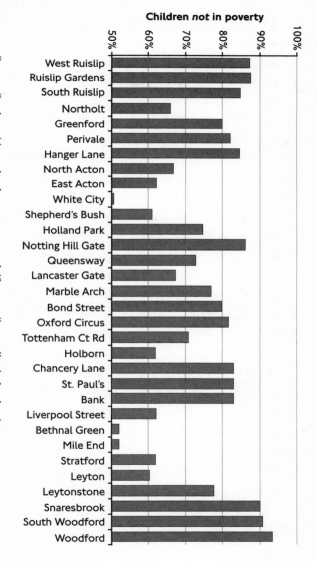

Children *not* in poverty

Source: See http://www.londonmapper.org.uk/features/inequality-in-london/

City Estate and parts of Shepherd's Bush to the
west, places surrounded by riches on either side,
a high-turnover enclave for the few without
much to call home.

Here, and for many miles to the south and a
few to the north of the Central Line, poverty is
normal. But then, as we move up the line and out
towards Essex, very soon we come to stops where
less than one child in ten is living in poverty; we
soon come to the lowest rates found anywhere
along the line. Poverty is least common in the far
north-east of London, not – perhaps – where
you might have expected it to be most absent.
No great riches are found further out, but little
desperation either. And next, between there and
here, on the border, comes Leytonstone and the
last new beginning of life in this story of the line.

Leytonstone, 8.00 p.m.

He was going to be a great-grandfather. He
was 85 and his oldest granddaughter was 28.
She was very pregnant. He'd come over on
a ship from Jamaica. Not that ship, not the

one everyone talks about, but a troop ship
returning to Southampton. He had been 18 and
a stowaway. They found him after a day at sea
spent steaming back across the Atlantic, having
dropped the troops home in Kingston, Jamaica.

He'd got to London early, in the 1940s,
before it was that usual to see black men here,
apart from on the docks. It had been hard, but
it got better. However, he was worried for his
granddaughter. Her boyfriend wasn't working.
He was black too. He liked to think she'd
gone for him because he reminded her of her
grandfather. But the boy didn't have a job. It
was hard, he kept on thinking, without a job.
She'd said half the black men in Britain didn't
have a job, but could that be true?[93]

He lived on his own now, in sheltered housing.
He was reading a letter from a friend in Jamaica.
Some of his friends had gone back there, back to
retire. But he wanted to be near his family here.
He'd have liked to live with his family, but no
one did that any more (apparently).

He didn't like the word 'apparently'. He'd
noticed how the way people spoke was changing.
There had been a time when people had been

proud to speak according to where they were from, and then a time when they pretended to speak as if they were from Jamaica.

'*Rastafari*'. It made him laugh. But now youngsters were careful to try to talk better. They wanted to be winners. Only a few people got all the money. Most black men, young black men at least, were not seen as worth employing at all, even though over half lived in London, where everything was booming still. It was funny, that. It wasn't as if there wasn't enough money.

He could remember the 1980s. Just like now, half of all young black men had had no work. He had been at the end of his working life then. He was at the end of his retired life now. It had made him angry then, but not as angry as the younger ones. But he'd done OK. He'd bought his houses. Cheap houses in cheap places, but they'd gone up in value. That's why he could be here in his last years. Not somewhere cheaper and not so nice. It wasn't that he'd worked for it, just luck. He'd come at the right time, been in the right places. It made him sad now. His grandson-in-law-to-be had been unlucky. Perhaps the granddaughter and her boyfriend should emigrate?

Snaresbrook, 8.30 p.m.

In the care home at Snaresbrook they got the *Mirror* and the *Mail*. She always read the *Mirror* first, but there was more in the *Mail*. In the paper a well-off couple were complaining about losing their £20.30 Child Benefit per week, or the possibility of that. She'd never had that much money when she was bringing up the kids. It had been shillings and pence then. Full Family Allowances had not come in until the 1970s, she thought; she was not quite sure, but she knew it was after her kids had grown up, after decimalization. She was 87 now.

She could remember the children growing up. She often couldn't remember other things. Sometimes she thought they were humouring her. She caught them just agreeing with her to shut her up. They were trying to put her off going outside.

Where was she living? She'd been put in this home when she'd got too angry with her daughter. It wasn't really her choice. She knew there was a tube stop nearby. Could she get to that on foot? She thought it was her fault that they didn't visit. Maybe they were afraid of the area. Was it safe to park? Why didn't they come by tube? And £20.30 a week is a lot of money. She didn't really have much use for money now, but she wanted to leave them something.

What she'd really like to do would be to get out, just to get out of the home for a day, even half a day. She'd like to look around. She'd like to go on the tube. She'd like to know where she was, what kind of a neighbourhood this was. She'd like to have something other than the *Mirror* or *Mail* to read at weekends. She'd like a different set of people at supper time for conversation or at least just a little different conversation. She didn't really want much.

It was a lot of money, £20.30, to spend on a child each and every week. They'll be spoilt, she thought. Someone used to come and get her and drive her to vote when there were elections, but that hadn't happened for years now. She'd always voted. She'd voted Labour in her first election, just like everyone else. She'd been 21, just after the war, just old enough to vote. They didn't know about the war, most people.

South Woodford, 9.00 p.m.

She put the magnifying glass down on the table and carefully placed the bookmark in the pages. She put the book next to the glass.

Getting out of the chair was the hardest part. Everything was easy after that. She had two sticks. She was very careful to ensure that they were placed within reach where they could not be knocked over. If she knocked one over she was stuck, possibly stuck until Tuesday. She didn't like to think about that. She could crawl and find it, she thought. She wouldn't be stuck. Not if she were not hurt.

Slowly she levered herself out of the chair. It would have been easier if it were firmer. It had been a firmer chair long ago.

She liked having her old things around her. Even her commode was old now. Her most treasured possessions were the photographs. She thought the paper faded more quickly in the more recent photographs, a little like her memory. Maybe it was how they were printed nowadays; the paper was not the same. She had photographs of all her relatives. Last year they had all turned up for her 90th birthday party, but no one came for her birthday this year. At least things are better, she thought, better for the children.[94] But nothing had happened today.

Slowly she made her way across the room, two legs and two sticks. To balance, she always had to have at least three points touching the floor; one foot or one stick could move at any one time. Falling hurt, much more than it used to hurt.

The woman who came on Tuesdays to wash her was from Woodford, the assigned 'carer'. Her carer complained of not having enough money. At least that is what she thought the woman was complaining about. Her hearing was so bad and the woman spoke in a foreign accent, but she got to better understand it over time. She had to. Or maybe her carer was speaking more clearly, learning better English, becoming more confident, becoming less foreign.

Now she couldn't see so easily it was hard to read for long, but she had nothing else to do all day. When the carer told her of her aches and pains she joked back that aches and pains were how you knew you were still alive!

Sometimes she wished it was not so hard, although she wondered how people coped before and she didn't complain because of that. What did they do before stairlifts? What happened before there were any assigned carers? What had happened to her grandparents and great-grandparents? She sat and thought.

She would have liked to have had some more company, liked to have lived with relatives. But maybe they would just argue.

It took another 15 minutes to get from the stairlift to her bed. It then took another five minutes to get into bed.

She prayed and then, with some difficulty, went to sleep.

Woodford, 9.30pm

'Grandad's asleep,' she said.

Grandad lived with them. His money had made it possible for them to live here. The deal was that they gave him some company.

'Don't forget the baby,' he said.

How could she forget the baby? The baby

was the reason she'd had no sleep for the last three months. The baby was the reason they'd moved here from down the line. The baby was the reason that they were living with her grandad. They'd moved for the baby, for the extra room, for the future. The baby was much more important than the census form. The form had been sitting by the kitchen sink for a week.

'People always forget to add the baby,' he said. He worked in town, in Islington, he changed at Bank, but in May the office was moving to Pimlico and then he'd change at Oxford Circus.[95] That was the great thing about the Central Line: it didn't matter if you changed your job or if your job changed its offices – everything was always the same distance away.

They'd moved here because it was safe and getting safer. Crime in the ward was the lowest for miles around, just five crimes for every 1,000 people a year (it would drop by another 15 per cent this year). What crime there was there was mostly petty antisocial behaviour. More of it took place in sub-ward 'E01003746' than anywhere else.

'That's why we didn't choose to live there,' he said.[96]

He liked statistics. He worked for the Office for National Statistics. On the tube it took him exactly 21 minutes to do *The Times* crossword, leaving precisely a minute to sit down in his seat and precisely a minute to get up.

'People don't know that this end of the line is better value,' he told her. She had wanted him to mortgage them to the hilt to secure them a premier postcode in West Ruislip (at the other end of the Central Line), a place where the average GCSE score was only 356 points.[97]

He had tried to explain it all to her when they were looking at possible semis there. 'But our child won't be average; our child will be very clever. Here, in Monkhams, the average is a whole 8 points higher!' He had lost her attention.

'Babies get left off census forms all the time,' he had said that morning. 'I told someone at work yesterday, someone who lives in West Ruislip. But here's better for schools.'[98]

'We shouldn't be choosing where to live because of statistics,' she said.

'No,' he agreed, and then spoilt it. 'Exactly two minutes down the line at South Woodford, the GCSE point average is 351. Slipping by more than a whole grade in one subject,' he said, as she rolled her eyes at him.

'Hasn't Grandad been asleep a long time?' he asked.

Leytonstone to Woodford

Even though child poverty is lowest along this final stretch of the line in London, life expectancy is not particularly high. There are a large number of old people in London, but mostly in outer London. Older people tend to get out of London altogether if they can and most get out at least as far as Essex. Those that are left within the Greater London boundary tend, on average, to live a few months or years less than the residents of many places to be found a little further north and west. More importantly, there is no great influx of life's more elderly and established winners into this part of the line. People who have won in the short term are here, but far fewer of the offspring of wealthier families, far fewer who

Life expectancy

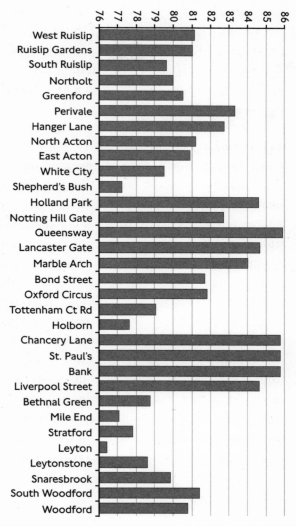

began life on the winning sides. Here are far more who are still on a journey.

Migrants and their offspring who have secured a toehold in London often end up moving towards this part of town, as well also as people who think of themselves as being more 'London' than others. They are often more 'London' because they have to go back three or four generations to identify the first immigrant in their family history and can find no university graduates more than just one generation ago.

The very highest longevity on the line is found as it cuts through the heart of the Royal Borough of Kensington and Chelsea, just north of the royal palaces. But almost as high are the rates on the Central Line in the financial heart of the City. Three tube stops in the graph above have the same life expectancy. This is because more precise figures for the immediate areas surrounding them are not available.

The drop in expected length of life from Bank to Leyton is ten years in just 14 minutes spent on the tube. It would be hard to find anywhere else within Europe where such large populations live so near to each other and yet one group gets to enjoy, each on average, an extra decade of a far more pampered life. If London divides more in future we will measure it in the number of extra breaths taken by those who bring home an even greater share of all the wealth that the capital corrals.

The Central Line doesn't end at Woodford. It continues out of London. It splits. It loops. And it merges into the worldwide network of metropolitan, national and international arteries.

No single transect from one edge of an urban boundary to the other can summarize the gradients that sustain and subvert people's cooperation. The working of the metropolis, this collective human organ, is made up of millions more people. Carry on out and the furthest-flung commuter villages enter its workings. Continue further out and you get to the supporting hinterland, to the places from where monies are raised by London firms, to areas where those deemed to have failed in London are rehoused.

London is one of the cities at the peak of a global metropolitan hierarchy so dependent on financial reassurance that ultimately that hierarchy, and its hinterlands, allow people in London to live like they do. From the broadcasters in the west to the bankers in the east, from Holland Park mansions to Mile End maisonettes, from the impoverished slums in every corner of the earth to a few shimmering office blocks holding extraordinary influence and power, the Central Line runs under the heart of it all.

Endnote, 10.00 p.m.

When were you last on the Central Line? Many Londoners have their stories of the line. For huge numbers of people, significant parts of their lives have been spent commuting along it. Within London, population turnover is so high, and commuting so extensive, that millions think on themselves as commuters or former commuters on the line. Millions more have used it to go shopping, to see the sights, to visit friends. Many people visiting from abroad have travelled on it and millions more have used it in past decades.

The 32 London stops on the Central Line

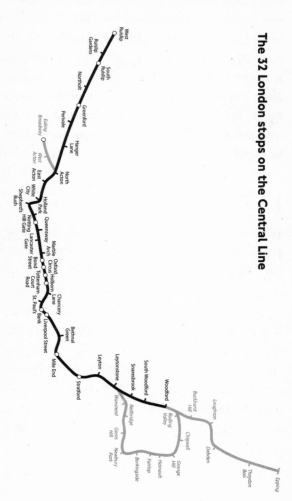

To add colour to this story of the human geography of one part of the tube, local facts have been added. All these are referenced in short notes listed below. Government and local authority press releases and news-sheets have been perused. Local ward 'neighbourhood news' reports are well worth reading and are also referenced below. Very often these are deposited on the Internet. Each of the 32 tube stops along the Central Line that lie within the Greater London boundary either falls within a ward or is most closely associated with a particular ward or, only very occasionally, a small group of wards. These are the places this book has been about, these wards by the tube stops, and the people who sleep in them, who live by the line and wake up along it: nearly half a million individuals, a population similar to that of the City of Sheffield, but stretched out to be living alongside London's most striking line, the red one, the one that looks like a heartbeat.

Notes

1. Life expectancy in West Ruislip is reported to be 81.1361 years; in Northolt Mandeville ward it is 79.9763 years. Travel time is seven minutes. To be precise, that is one day and 11 minutes of life lost per second spent moving east on the train. The source of this data is 'Ward level life expectancy estimates for the period 2005–2009 (data combined)', Greater London Authority, 2011. See http://data.london.gov.uk/.

2. All the sources used in this book are freely accessible on the web. Although I use it sparingly here, by far the best source of all is Wikipedia. Like all sources, you have to cross-check Wikipedia. Unlike others, you can

correct it and then others can correct you if they see fit. See http://en.wikipedia.org/wiki/Census_in_the_United_Kingdom.

3. 'ONS moves to new London office', press release, 16 May 2011. See http://www.ons.gov.uk/ons/media-centre/statements/ons-moves-to-new-london-office.html.

4. This is in sub-ward 'E01002535', according to the Metropolitan Police. Google that nine-character code to find out more and to see where people like us quantitative social geographers get some of our information from.

5. Metropolitan Police Crime Statistics, West Ruislip annual crime count, 2008–9, 2009–10, 2010–11: 928, 807 and 690 respectively. See http://maps.met.police.uk/access.php?area=00ASHC&sort=area.

6. Capped GCSE average point scores for pupils at the end of Key Stage 4 in maintained schools (referenced by location of pupil residence) based on ward-level data for 2010 (Greater London Authority, 2011). For more details of the fascinating world of GCSE scoring, turn to the conversation taking place later on in the

semi-fictional day that this book describes, in Woodford at 9.30 p.m., and the footnotes to that.

7. West Ruislip Ward Profile, Hillingdon NHS Primary Care Trust. An update is due once the 2011 results are released in 2013. For now, as published in July 2007, table labelled: 'Proportion of Ethnic Communities: 1991 and 2001 West Ruislip' (wrongly implying 90 per cent of residents have no ethnicity – we all have an ethnicity). See http://hillingdon.nhs.uk/uploads/Ward%20profiles/West%20Ruislip%20July%202006R.pdf.

8. 'A focus on Manor Ward', Hillingdon Policy Team, January 2010 (the nearest tube stop to Manor is Ruislip Gardens): 5,203 of the 10,797 residents of this ward are said to be in the 'Acorn' groups labelled 'post-industrial families'. See http://www.hillingdon.gov.uk/media/pdf/3/0/Manor_10.pdf.

9. 'A focus on Manor Ward', as above. 'Table: Educational Attainment of Pupils', 2007, 2008, 2009.

10. 'A focus on South Ruislip Ward', Corporate Performance & Intelligence Team, April 2011,

map on p. 15. See http://www.hillingdon.gov.uk/
media/pdf/2/e/South_Ruislip_2011.pdf.

11. 'A focus on South Ruislip', Policy Team, January
2010. See http://www.hillingdon.gov.uk/media/
pdf/5/b/South_Ruislip_10.pdf.

12. HMRC, 2007–8, 'WTC 1 – Child Tax Credit
and Working Tax Credit: An introduction'.
See www.hmrc.gov.uk/pdfs/wtc1.pdf.

13. Shelter's estimate of the drop in allowances
to help pay the rent for a three-bed property
in Hillingdon in April 2011: p. 9 of their table
here. See http://england.shelter.org.uk/campaigns/
housing_issues/local_housing_allowance.

14. When riots did take place in Ealing that
summer most of that rioting occurred within a
few hundred metres of Ealing Broadway tube
station, on the spur of the Central Line not
included in this transect. Of the 137 people
arrested in Ealing, 122 were male; some
39 were 'young'. Half of those lived in the
borough. See 'The Ealing Riots: the Council's
Response & Recovery', 13 September 2011.
And for more detail see also http://www2.ealing.
gov.uk/ealing3/export/sites/ealingweb/services/
council/committees/agendas_minutes_reports/

ward_forums/northolt_west_end_ward_forum/_
april2011-march2012/_13_October_2011/Ealing_
Riots_-_Briefing_Note.pdf

15. The speed of the trains varies on different lines,
on different parts of each line and at different
times of day, as well as when there are more
or fewer trains. But speed is hard to gauge
when there is almost nothing to see out of the
windows.

16. Everything matters, even that cigarette, the one
the man from South Ruislip finally had at 9 a.m.
this morning, when our tale reaches Hanger
Lane. Everything is influenced by everything
else, but nearby things are more related than
distant things. See http://en.wikipedia.org/wiki/
Tobler's_first_law_of_geography.

17. See http://www.londonmapper.org.uk/features/
inequality-in-london/ for the data sources for
these charts. They were drawn with the help
of Benjamin Hennig, who created that website
with me for the Trust for London, and then
redrawn by Paul Coles.

18. 'Greenford Green Ward Priorities', Greenford
Green Neighbourhood News, Issue 1,
January 2011, p. 2. See http://www2.ealing.

gov.uk/ealing3/export/sites/ealingweb/services/
council/committees/agendas_minutes_reports/
ward_forums/greenford_green_ward_forum/_
april10-march11/28_October_2010/Greenford_
Green_newsletter_Jan_2011.pdf.

19. 'What matters to you in your ward?', *Perivale Neighborhood News*, Issue 2, January 2009, p. 1 (box). See http://www2.ealing.gov.uk/ealing3/export/ sites/ealingweb/services/council/committees/ agendas_minutes_reports/ward_forums/ perivale_ward_forum/_sept08-may09/_26jan09/ Ward_Newsletter_-_Perivale_Jan_09_to_print.pdf.

20. 'Deterring anti social behaviour in Bilton Road and beyond', *Perivale Neighbourhood News*, Issue 1, December 2010, p. 1. (Note that Issue 1 comes almost two years after Issue 2!) Read all about it at http://www2.ealing.gov. uk/ealing3/export/sites/ealingweb/services/ council/committees/agendas_minutes_reports/ ward_forums/perivale_ward_forum/_april10- march11/_5_October_2010/EC2627_Ward_ Newsletter_Perivale_web.pdf.

21. Presumably they don't welcome people with open arms who would like to see the

social landscape become a little less uneven: Ealing Central & Acton Conservatives, 'Introduction to Hanger Hill Ward'. See http://www.ealingactonconservatives.org. uk/your-area/hanger-hill.

22. In fact, some parts of the Conservative Party pay London Letterbox Marketing to deliver its leaflets as the party cannot find enough volunteers willing to give up time but it does have enough money from just a few of its wealthy donors. On how paying companies to deliver political leaflets can cause problems in London see http://www.thisislocallondon.co.uk/ news/9652399.Political_war_on_streets_of_Bromley_ over_leaflet_delivery/.

23. All these conversations took place on 2 April 2011. Just a year later the idea of £9,000-a-year university fees had become widely accepted. People often quickly adjust to the circumstances they find themselves in. Few people thought of the imposition of such high fees on the young as a form of antisocial behaviour. However, once 'interest' is added the amount to be paid back is far higher than £27,000. And the future interest

rate can be changed at any time, by the relevant
Secretary of State, without any need for new
legislation.

24. Down by Ealing and West London College,
    next to Ealing Studios, or down by the 'Local'
    supermarket on Ealing Green. In other words,
    where there was rioting later in August 2011.
    See http://www2.ealing.gov.uk/ealing3/export/
    sites/ealingweb/services/council/committees/
    agendas_minutes_reports/ward_forums/northolt_
    west_end_ward_forum/_april2011-march2012/_13_
    October_2011/Ealing_Riots_-_Briefing_Note.pdf.

25. And a mile (1,650 metres to be exact) of
    'retaining structure', whatever that means.
    The plans for the station can be found at http://
    assets.dft.gov.uk/publications/hs2-maps-20120110/
    hs2arp00drrw05002issue3.pdf.

26. R. Razaq, 'We need HS2 tunnel too, say residents',
    Evening Standard, 23 January 2012. See http://www.
    thisislondon.co.uk/standard/article-24029998-we-
    need-hs2-tunnel-too-say-residents.do.

27. Further down the line it is the 33-year-old
    in Holland Park who will give birth at 34.
    Meanwhile the 49-year-old daughter of the
    grandmother we'll meet in Bethnal Green is

about to become a mother for the third time. If you could compare the families of all the babies born in the capital in just one day the snapshot would illustrate how massively socially split this city has become. Even along one tube line people live in different worlds. To the east of the Central Line it is not unusual for many mothers to still have living grandmothers or even great-grandmothers.

28. The ages of all the mothers along the line are 19, 23, 25, 28, 29, 32, 34, 38, 42 and 49. These numbers were drawn from the distribution given in official publications for England and Wales, extrapolating forward seven years from 2004 based on the trend from 1997 to 2004. See 'Maternities: Age of mother, 1938–2004, a. all maternities', itself taken from Table 3.4 published in *Birth Statistics* 1837–1983, Historical series FM1, Vol. 13, and from Table 3.2 published in *Birth Statistics* 1837–1983, Historical series FM1, Vols. 11–33 (Office of National Statistics, London).

29. Later on in this story it is grandchildren who will become parents at ages 19, 23, 25 and 28. These four all live between Mile End and

Leytonstone (inclusive). However, most adults who live towards the centre of the Central Line are not parents and many will never be. London is where people are least likely to have children and, if they have them, to have them at older ages. The parents in the western end of north-west London would have had to have been older still, on average, for the age profile to be representative of the capital as it is today.

30. See http://www.tfl.gov.uk/tfl/tickets/faresand tickets/farefinder/current/default.aspx. Last time she had to visit it had been Feltham and she took the Piccadilly Line to Heathrow. It had been £5.30 one way then. For some reason an Oyster would only save you 50p on that trip. She was travelling from Bethnal Green.

31. She didn't learn it from the Internet, as she didn't have access and wouldn't know how to work the Web if she did. It is at http://www.justice.gov.uk/global/contacts/noms/prison-finder/wormwood-scrubs/visiting-information.htm.

32. He got caught again later that year in August. Like fish thrown back in the river, some are better at getting caught than others: BBC,

'One in four riot suspects had 10 previous offences', 15 September 2011. See http://www.bbc.co.uk/news/uk-14926322.

33. A. Foster (show-business correspondent), 'BBC Breakfast's Sian Williams quits to escape move to Salford', *Evening Standard*, 29 March 2011. See http://www.thisislondon.co.uk/standard/article-23936344-bbc-breakfasts-sian-williams-quits-to-escape-move-to-salford.do.

34. Comment on above story by 'Adam, Lancashire, 30/03/2011, 10:12'.

35. '. . . the last half mile is wholly irrecoverable. The Central Line running north-west between White City and East Acton, and the A40, have cut off the runners' access route from DuCane Road, and there is nothing left of the stadium': M. Pooley, 'From Windsor Castle to White City: The 1908 Olympic Marathon Route', *London Journal*, Vol. 34, No. 2, July 2009, p. 176. See http://eprints.soton.ac.uk/65679/1/LDN4206.pdf.

36. Among the exhibits in White City in 1911 a 'Somali village was found in the shadow of the Mountain Railway. They were headed by Mohamed, who had acted as a British interpreter during the campaign against the

Mad Mullah.' See http://www.studygroup.org.uk/
Exhibitions/Pages/1911%20Coronation.htm.

37. 'Council elections 2010 Wormholt and
White City ward' given by Hammersmith
and Fulham Council. See http://www.lbhf.
gov.uk/Directory/Council_and_Democracy/
Democracy_and_Elections/Electoral_services/
Useful_links/142724_Council_elections_2010_
Wormholt_and_White_City_ward.asp.

38. 'Off the Track in London', published in 1911,
described the area as 'the Avernus of Kensington',
the gateway to hell. It was said then to have the
'Highest Death Rate in London', in St Clements'
parish magazine. See p. 3 of http://www.
historytalk.org/Notting%20Dale/NDnotes1.pdf.

39. See Notting Hill History Timeline at:
http://www.historytalk.org/Notting%20Dale/
timelinechap4.pdf.

40. Among the anarchists, George Sims noted in
1904 that 'there are odd ones holding socialistic
and revolutionary doctrines . . . but as to the
majority of my people, I have been deeply
touched, at times, to see how firmly rooted the
King and Queen are in the affections of even
the most depraved and violent', *History Talk*,

Issue 13, November/December 2008, p. 4. See
http://www.historytalk.org/Notting%20Dale/
Newsletter13.pdf.

41. See http://www.historytalk.org/Notting%20Dale/
NDnotes1.pdf.

42. The Great Western. All this is according to
George Sims, in 1904 and published again in
1911. See p. 7 of http://www.historytalk.org/
Notting%20Dale/NDnotes1.pdf.

43. Same source, referring in turn to 'London City
Mission Magazine, October 1911'.

44. 'One in Ten' by UB40 reached number one
in the charts in August 1981. The history of
all UB40 songs is graphed here: http://www.
chartstats.com/artistinfo.php?id=667. 'Gangsta's
Paradise' reached number one in the UK in
1995. Its progress can be seen at http://www.
chartstats.com/songinfo.php?id=23489.

45. D. Dorling, R. Garside and N. Kerrison, 'Young
adults in transition: the local picture in national
context', Centre for Crime and Justice Studies,
Briefing 12, 2011. See http://www.dannydorling.
org/?page_id=2931.

46. 'Children with a Parent in Prison Conference:
Impact, Issues, Practice and Policy', The Sherwell

Centre, Plymouth University, United Kingdom,
Monday 2 April 2012. See http://www.plymouth.
ac.uk/pages/view.asp?page=37922.

47. The original source for the 7 per cent figure
is the New Labour Green Paper 'Every
Child Matters'. See http://www.education.
gov.uk/consultations/downloadableDocs/
EveryChildMatters.pdf. On p. 43 it states: 'Seven
percent of children during their time at school
experience the imprisonment of a father, while
every year, approximately 150,000 children have
a parent who enters custody.' Thanks to Eleanor
Carter of the University of Sheffield for finding
this source when I could not remember where I
had first heard of it or seen it!

48. By 2012 the minimum that a single adult
needed, living alone, for a basic but minimally
decent life was £193 a week after their rent,
tax and National Insurance were paid. Just to
get by on what was deemed the same – very
minimal – standard, a couple with children
aged three and seven needed £455 a week after
those essential costs were met and childcare
costs were included for when both adults
were working. If both adults were working,

then they would each need to earn £18,400 a
year to reach that minimal level of decency.
All the families with children labelled as poor
here in White City were living on far less
than even that amount. See http://www.jrf.org.
uk/focus-issue/minimum-income-standards.

49. Life expectancy is always an average and wealth
does not always infer health. In July 2012 the
body of billionairess Eva Rausing was found
in her mansion, just over a mile (across some
of the most expensive real estate in the world)
from Holland Park. Earlier she and her husband
had been photographed looking 'gaunt and
dishevelled' as they tried to leave their home
incognito. Not all is well for the rich and
especially not for the extremely rich. See http://
www.mirror.co.uk/news/uk-news/eva-rausing-dead-
wife-of-tetra-1139778.

50. See http://www.thisislondon.co.uk/standard/article-
23983968-ex-councillor-faces-child-porn-charges.do.

51. See http://www.movielocationsguide.com/Notting_
Hill/filming_locations/House_With_Blue_Door.php.

52. See http://www.rbkc.gov.uk/electionmap/atlas.
html. Colville returned two Liberal and one
Labour councillors in May 2010. To the north

and west all wards were Labour in that borough, to the south all were Tory.

53. Later revealed in the *Evening Standard*: A. Davis, 'Three boroughs to merge libraries in an attempt to stave off closures', 17 June 2011. See http://www.thisislondon.co.uk/standard/ article-23961506-three-boroughs-to-merge-libraries-in-an-attempt-to-stave-off-closures.do.

54. It kept on happening: R. Cooper, 'Gone off the rails: Porsche left balancing precariously over ledge after smashing through metal fence', *Daily Mail*, 3 February 2012. See http://www.dailymail. co.uk/news/article-2096179/Porsche-left-balancing-precariously-ledge-smashing-railings-crash.html.

55. William Wales studied history of art, but that subject turned out to be a little too complex, so, unlike the woman who later became his wife, he switched degrees to the more convivial study of geography. It is an academic discipline that's also useful given all the place names in his official title: His Royal Highness Prince William Arthur Philip Louis, Duke of Cambridge, Earl of Strathearn, Baron Carrickfergus, Royal Knight Companion of the Most Noble Order of the Garter.

56. See http://www.onehydepark.com/#/index and http://www.onehydepark.com/downloads/pdf/ adib-brochure.pdf. Which continues: 'Occupying a prime location within the newly completed One Hyde Park development adjacent to Rolex and McLaren retail flagship stores'.

57. When he was coming here he'd googled 'Hyde Park' and come up with a street in what looked like a council estate in Wakefield, West Yorkshire, just by the sewage works. It probably wasn't a council estate; coming from the States, he didn't have the eye to distinguish between maisonettes and two-ups, two-downs: 1 Hyde Park Wakefield, West Yorkshire WF1 4ET. Anyway – he was learning quickly. He wouldn't be here for long; maybe they'd move him to a self-catering but serviced apartment in Chelsea if his posting was for a few more months, and then they could save a little on the rent here. It just wasn't healthy having all your food delivered by room service – but at least the portions were small (by American standards).

58. City of Westminster: Bryanston and Dorset Square ward, ONS Government Statistical Service Code E05000632. A decade ago, within

exactly 6,677 dwellings, some 10,669 people lived in this area, 37.5 years old on average, hardly any children or pensioners, but 163 Buddhists. For full details, including a nice map, see http://openlylocal.com/wards/1670-Bryanston-and-Dorset-Square.

59. Let's say it's St Edward's RC Primary School, Unique Reference Number (URN): 101128, Lisson Grove, London NW1 6LH. On the 36 languages see http://www.ofsted.gov.uk/provider/files/916555/urn/101128.pdf.

60. A little later in time the map of multiple deprivation would be found at http://mappinglondon.co.uk/2012/02/13/the-index-of-multiple-deprivation-as-a-map/.

61. Or at least the local Conservative Party does call it a village despite it being in London. See http://www.westminsterconservatives.co.uk/node/69.

62. B. Barrow and L. Farndon, 'Greed "is good": Anger as Barclays bosses hand themselves up to £47m a head in pay and bonuses – and then claim it's in best interests of Britain', *Daily Mail*, 8 March 2011. See http://www.dailymail.co.uk/

news/article-1363790/Barclays-bosses-47m-head-pay-bonuses-Bob-Diamond-says-greed-good.html.

63. See the 'Daily Mail Song' at http://www.youtube.com/watch?v=5eBT6OSr1TI.

64. He's stopped using that line since Bob Diamond was let go in conditions of infamy and Jerry had to resign and was called to explain his actions in the UK and USA (where a criminal inquiry was being considered): P. Inman, 'Ex-Barclays executive to be grilled by MPs over Libor scandal', *Guardian*, 15 July 2012. See http://www.guardian.co.uk/business/2012/jul/15/barclays-jerry-del-missier-libor.

65. 'Rebekah Brooks visits Rupert Murdoch's London home for talks – Rupert Murdoch meets News International chief executive Rebekah Brooks and chairman James Murdoch after arriving in the UK to take personal charge of the phone-hacking scandal engulfing his business', *Guardian*, 11 July 2011. See http://www.guardian.co.uk/media/video/2011/jul/11/rebekah-brooks-rupert-murdoch-video.

66. He'd been given access to the data early, before Camden Council released it to the

public as Camden Data's 'Bloomsbury ward general health profile 2011/12', release date 17 August 2011. See http://www.camdendata.info/AddDocuments1/Forms/DispForm.aspx?ID=310.

67. First page of 'Bloomsbury ward general health profile 2011/12' referenced above, in note 66.

68. A Veblen good is a type of positional good where 'preference for buying them increases as their price increases, as greater price confers greater status'. See http://en.wikipedia.org/wiki/Veblen_good. Almost all goods have been of this type at one time or another. See http://www.evolutionary-economics.org/KSH-Postings-Econ/178.html.

69. Within Camden 'Holborn and Covent Garden ward has the most accommodation located in commercial buildings (9%) and the second highest proportion of accommodation with lowest floor level being 5th floor or above (13%). It has the second highest proportion of purpose-built flats (70%), ranks 2nd for resident workers who walk to work (37%) and ranks 3rd lowest on the proportion of households owning cars (31%). The ward has the second highest proportion of people living

alone (54% of households)', 2001 Census Ward Profiles Holborn and Covent Garden, January 2007. See http://www.camden.gov.uk/ccm/content/council-and-democracy/about-the-council/camden-statistics/census-test-2007/file-storage-items/ward-profile--holborn-and-covent-garden.en.

70. See previous note. When the 2011 small area census data is released we shall probably find that the proportion of people living alone has risen to be even higher, despite the astronomical cost of property there rising so quickly. If demand and supply ever balanced these properties would be crowded.

71. Ten months later newspaper journalists began to write that: 'At the beginning of the crisis, wealthy Greeks, often hauling suitcases of cash, flew to the UK where they snapped up prime properties in central London, so much so that estate agents called them the "new Arabs"', H. Smith, 'Greek fears grow beneath looming shadow of bankruptcy', *Guardian*, 17 February 2012. See http://www.guardian.co.uk/world/2012/feb/17/greece-crisis-fears-bankruptcy.

72. It may be that the depth of the fall in life expectancy in the stops towards Holborn is less

topical because the height the fall is from is greater and so life expectancy does not become quite so low as in the East End. Travelling west to east, the only steeper descent is the six years of life lost in the three minutes from Liverpool Street to Bethnal Green. Per metre travelled rather than per second the gradient is steeper along Oxford Street.

73. Cities of London and Westminster Conservative Association, Marylebone High Street Ward webpage at http://www.westminsterconservatives. co.uk/node/69.

74. Holborn and St Pancras Conservative Association, Holborn and Covent Garden Ward, 4 April 2011. See http://hspca.org. uk/2011/04/04/labour-councillor-forces-young-family-to-leave-home/.

75. What you need to keep in your mind, when reading about the City of London, is why they never say on their websites when it is that people get to vote for the local government of the area, or why the elected Mayor of London has no real power over this small part of the capital where so much of the wealth and power really is. See http://www.cityoflondon.gov.uk/Corporation/

LGNL_Services/Council_and_democracy/
Council_departments/whatis.htm.

76. Read the riveting 'Farringdon Without Ward
News'. Earlier copies appear to be unavailable,
but Issue 22 is at http://www.cityoflondon.gov.uk/
committees/ward_newsletters/22.pdf.

77. 'The Square Mile houses some of the richest
concentrations of economic activity in the
world. However, its neighbours include some
of the UK's most deprived communities. The
City of London Corporation is acutely aware
that the City should not prosper in isolation
and is therefore committed to working with
partners in the public, private and voluntary
sectors to bring lasting social, economic and
physical regeneration to the City fringes.
The City of London is actively engaged in
numerous regeneration partnerships and also
contributes funding to a wide range . . .' For
more, and a picture of six black people they
have helped (or at least that is the very tacky
implication of the image) see http://www.
cityoflondon.gov.uk/Corporation/LGNL_Services/
Environment_and_planning/Regeneration/.

78. Z. Saeed, 'St Paul's Cathedral marks 300th anniversary', *BBC News*, 4 March 2011. See http://www.bbc.co.uk/news/uk-england-london-12635948.

79. Shirley Williams was 80 at the time of this encounter. The book her pacifist mother, Vera Brittain, wrote was entitled *Testament of Youth*. On the meeting that Shirley was attending, see Ekklesia, 'A New Way of Thinking', 29 March 2011: http://www.ekklesia.co.uk/node/14437. Ekklesia is affiliated to the Robin Hood Tax Campaign. Almost a year later: 'Christians are continuing plans for a ring of prayer at the eviction of Occupy London Stock Exchange, even if the bailiffs are sent in at night-time. The Court of Appeal today [22 February] ruled in favour of the eviction of the camp, meaning it could now take place at any time.' See http://www.ekklesia.co.uk/node/16309. See also http://londonist.com/2011/03/tonight-robin-hood-tax-debate-at-st-pauls-cathedral.php on other reports of that meeting. In contrast to these two reports, tens of thousands of stories were posted about the Occupy camp. The camp was cleared late on the night of 27 February 2012.

80. '. . . when hard paste porcelain was reproduced in imitation of Chinese originals in the 1760s, those able to afford the latest "china" demonstrated their social superiority by adding the tea first and the milk afterwards', Andrew, Bristol, England: http://www.guardian.co.uk/ notesandqueries/query/0,,-1400,00.html.

81. Sometimes there is no decent substitute for Wikipedia: see http://en.wikipedia.org/wiki/ Queenhithe.

82. The phrase would later appear in the December 2011 edition of the newsletter of another City ward – see http://www.cityoflondon.gov.uk/ committees/ward_newsletters/22.pdf – where it was used by a City Councilman to condemn the protesters at the cathedral. Maybe he had heard the phrase first at a dinner in April and it had stuck in his mind? The Councilman was a 'founding Director of the civil liberties group Big Brother Watch'. A group concerned partly with people looking too closely into the affairs of the City?

83. Such incidents happen all the time. A few months later one was filmed in January 2012: 'A suspect is arrested after video footage emerges

of a woman apparently abusing ethnic minority passengers on a Tube'. See http://www.bbc.co.uk/go/em/fr/-/news/uk-england-london-16932948. The YouTube clip could be found at http://www.youtube.com/watch?v=QCtqvOwLUNs&feature=related.

84. G. Monbiot, 'Britain is being rebuilt in aid of corporate power', *Guardian*, 27 February 2012. See http://www.guardian.co.uk/commentisfree/2012/feb/27/britain-rebuilt-in-aid-corporate-power?.

85. See chart on child poverty under 'Bethnal Green to Leyton', below (p. 117).

86. See chart of GCSE results shown just before Notting Hill Gate earlier on in this book (p. 50). This station and the next two have the lowest rates on the line, but still much higher scores than entire cities like Norwich, places not benefiting from London's pull of migrants, London's diversity of provision, and London's aggregated human energy.

87. See the chart of average incomes shown just before Chancery Lane tube stop above (p. 85).

88. See P. Thane and T. Evans, *Sinners? Scroungers? Saints? Unmarried Motherhood in Twentieth-century England* (Oxford, Oxford University Press, 2012)

and http://www.historyandpolicy.org/research/
new-books/newbook_11.html.

89. She's right, she's good with figures; although
women do get to live, on average, a little longer.
See the chart under 'Leytonstone to Woodford',
below (p. 129).

90. Quite where she read it is a mystery, but the
story surfaced again a few months later. 'And
there's been a shift in the nature of that wealth:
15 years ago, 75% of the Sunday Times Rich
List had inherited their wealth, and 25% were
self-made. Those figures are now reversed',
J. Henley, 'The new philanthropists', *Guardian*,
7 March 2012. See http://gu.com/p/362f9.

91. Many still call it that, but today it officially goes
by the name 'Queen Mary', having dropped
the less prestigious part of its former title. See
http://www.qmul.ac.uk/.

92. See http://en.wikipedia.org/wiki/Leyton_(ward) as
of 22 March 2012.

93. J. Ball, D. Milmo and B. Ferguson, 'Half of
UK's young black males are unemployed',
Guardian, 10 March 2012. See http://www.
guardian.co.uk/society/2012/mar/09/half-uk-
young-black-men-unemployed.

94. There was no way she could have known it, but around here just under a tenth were still living in poverty. Only a couple of miles up the line child poverty hit a minimum at Woodford.

95. 'ONS moves to new London office', press release, 16 May 2011. See http://www.ons.gov.uk/ons/media-centre/statements/ons-moves-to-new-london-office.html.

96. Metropolitan Police Crime Statistics, Monkhams' annual crime count, 2008–9, 2009–10, 2010–11: 534, 562 and 505 respectively. See http://maps.met.police.uk/php/dataview.php?area=00BCGN&ct=8&sort=rate&order=d.

97. These are capped GCSE average point scores for pupils at the end of Key Stage 4 in maintained schools based on ward-level data for 2010 (referenced by location of pupil residence, calculated by the Greater London Authority, 2011). Later he would try to explain the numbers to her with an example: 'The average child in London is awarded 337 points for their GCSEs. These points are for the eight highest marks each child is awarded. Suppose our child gained A*, A, B, C, C, C, D and E for their best eight GCSEs, that would equal 338 = 58 + 52 +

46 + 40 + 40 + 40 + 34 + 28 points. Now, suppose that D became an A, worth 52 points rather than 34, exactly 18 points extra, a new total of 356! That's the average at the other end of the tube, for West Ruislip.' In turn she replied, 'I thought no child gets both an A* and an E. Isn't that the point of streaming?' They then argued a little about what the difference between setting and streaming might be and which side of their respective families might have the 'better genes'. These were genes that, in his view, would show through in A*s. In her view it was more nurture than nature, as, if it were genes, wouldn't intelligence be inherited, like skin colour? When Grandad had been younger he'd told them he'd fought battles in the streets of London against people who believed such things, but now Grandad was lying stock still, having just died in his sleep above their heads in the room that would soon be repainted as the new nursery, just as they were forgetting his stories of the East End in the 1930s, of the Blackshirts, eugenics, of fighting prejudice and for a common good. Stories he would never be able to tell to his great-grandchild.

98. He was going to add that here there was not 'too much multiculturism', but he stopped himself. He knew she would disapprove of his prejudice, but he thought that it had an effect on the schools. 'Only about 11% of the population are from the Black Minority Group', Census 2001, Statistics and latest data on Monkhams, London Borough of Redbridge, Policy Teams, Strategic Services. See http://www2.redbridge.gov.uk/cms/the_council/about_the_council/about_redbridge/research_and_statistics/idoc. ashx?docid=abe3083c-55e2-4a23-b2bd-36e02b18of23&version=-1.

Acknowledgements

Thanks to Ruth Alexander, Helen Conford, Stacy Hewitt, Carl Lee, Bill Lodge, Bethan Thomas, Mary Wells and Amber Wilson, who all commented on earlier drafts. Thanks also to Benjamin Hennig, who pulled out the statistics used here, to Paul Coles, who redrew the diagrams, to Lesley Levene, who edited the text, to Rebecca Lee, who managed the production, to Helen Conford (again), who commissioned the book, to my agent, Ant Harwood, who persuaded her that this was a good idea, and to the Trust for London, which funded the research project that Ben and I were working on to map the social geography of the capital when the idea of this book was first proposed. I am also grateful to all those individuals who have assembled so many facts about London and published so many of them in online form. A selection can be found in the notes above.

PENGUIN LINES
Choose Your Journey

If you're looking for...

Romantic Encounters

Heads and Straights
by Lucy Wadham
(the Circle line)

Waterloo–City, City–Waterloo
by Leanne Shapton
(the Waterloo & City line)

Tales of Growing Up and Moving On

Heads and Straights
by Lucy Wadham
(the Circle line)

A Good Parcel of English Soil
by Richard Mabey
(the Metropolitan line)

Mind the Child
by Camila Batmanghelidjh and Kids Company
(the Victoria line)

The 32 Stops
by Danny Dorling
(the Central line)

Mind the Child
by Camila Batmanghelidjh
and Kids Company
(the Victoria line)

The Blue Riband
by Peter York
(the Piccadilly line)

**A Bit of
Politics**

The 32 Stops
by Danny Dorling
(the Central line)

*A History of Capitalism
According to the Jubilee Line*
by John O'Farrell
(the Jubilee line)

**Musical
Direction**

Heads and Straights
by Lucy Wadham
(the Circle line)

Earthbound
by Paul Morley
(the Bakerloo line)

The Blue Riband
by Peter York
(the Piccadilly line)

Tube Knowledge

What We Talk About When We Talk About The Tube
by John Lanchester
(the District line)

A Good Parcel of English Soil
by Richard Mabey
(the Metropolitan line)

A Breath of Fresh Air

A Good Parcel of English Soil
by Richard Mabey
(the Metropolitan line)

Design for Life

Waterloo—City, City—Waterloo
by Leanne Shapton
(the Waterloo & City line)

Buttoned-Up
by Fantastic Man
(the East London line)

Drift
by Philippe Parreno
(the Hammersmith & City line)